The Twelve-Year Sentence

The Twelve-

1974

Open Court

LaSalle, Illinois 61301

Year Sentence

Edited by William F. Rickenbacker

Printed in the United States of America

The 12-year sentence.

Papers prepared for an education symposium sponsored by the Institute for Humane Studies and the Center for Independent Education held in Milwaukee, Wis., Nov. 16-18, 1972.
1. Education, Compulsory—United States—Congresses. I. Rickenbacker, William F. II. Institute for Humane Studies. III. Center for Independent Education.
LC131.T93   379'.23'0973   73-23107
ISBN 0-87548-152-3

CONTENTS

Editor's Note

The editor's hand has rested lightly on these papers. I have cut out some overlaps, some digressions, some passages intended for the symposium audience in particular. I have sought to make the style consistent through the six papers without doing violence to any one author's style. Each paper as it appears here has the final approval of its author.

In the editing, only one point arose that seemed to need comment. The original six papers used the phrases "compulsory education" and "compulsory schooling" as if they were almost always interchangeable (Professor West being perhaps the most consistent in distinguishing between them). Professor Rothbard, however, maintained that this "seemingly sophisticated distinction" is "not valid." Taking Rothbard's cue, I have used the phrase "compulsory schooling" throughout, replacing in scores of places the author's original phrase "compulsory education," and using that latter phrase only where the meaning is undeniably different from "schooling."

Rothbard's argument is that giving the government the power to compel people to become educated leads to a governmental definition of the content of education, governmental standards, governmental certificates, and all the trappings of compulsory "schooling." This is highly likely on the practical level but not necessarily so in theory. An interesting analogy, one that appears in these papers in another context, is with the parental duty to nourish one's child. The government, in every civilized country, does possess plenary powers in cases where parents fail to feed their children; but the government does not publish menus, establish standards, issue cooking certificates, and so on. Highly unlikely though it may be in practice, it is at least conceivable that a government might strongly encourage a certain educational outcome without actively administering the educational apparatus.

—William F. Rickenbacker

Introduction

Benjamin A. Rogge

Department of Economics, Wabash College

Compulsory schooling has come under increasing fire from the educationists themselves and from outside critics. From one end of the country to the other, the subject of schooling—whether it be busing, budgets, curricula, indoctrination, prayer, lunches, sex courses, tax sources—gives rise to bitter and endless controversy. Even such entrenched educationist groups as the National Education Association have begun to question the wisdom of compulsory attendance at school, mainly because the educationists are the first to face the problem of dealing with genuinely uncontrollable youngsters. Political controversy over education is on the rise. Intellectual controversy, in which this collection of studious papers will play a major role, is at fever pitch. No doubt we can look forward to a growing number of court cases involving the use of compulsion in schooling. The whole subject is ripe for fundamental rethinking.

To many who support compulsory schooling, the use of compulsion is necessary to bring up the young to respect and practice the virtues and customs of the society. To the critics of compulsory schooling, it is precisely this coercive intrusion of the collective into the life and mind of the individual that represents the most damnable feature of compulsory schooling. Admittedly, in one or two of the papers to follow, you will find some evidence of a willingness to put up with compulsion if only the "right people" can be put in charge. Also you will find some support of the appropriateness of social indoctrination of the young—but without the feature of governmental coercion.

But most of all, what you will find is a series of mature and scholarly explorations of the possibility that the emperor of compulsory, government-operated schooling is in fact riding his horse before the public in a state of absolute nakedness. One man approaches the topic with the materials of history, another the law, or economics, or professional education, or some mixture of all of these. Some come at it with the value sets and presuppositions of the conservative right, others of the anarcho-capitalist or traditional Liberal or New Left positions. You will find both Paul Goodman and Cardinal Newman quoted with approval. Most importantly, you will find here some challenging and thoughtful and intelligent conversation on the whole set of public issues raised by the general topic of compulsory schooling.

These papers were prepared for an education symposium in Milwaukee, Wisconsin, November 16-18, 1972.
The authors met to lead discussions on their respective
papers, which had been distributed several weeks before
the conferees convened.

The Institute for Humane Studies and the Center for
Independent Education co-sponsored the symposium.
Both organizations have had a vital interest in education
over the past several years—the Institute for Humane
Studies with the awarding of fellowships for the prepa-
ration of background studies in the history and philosophy of education, and the Center for Independent
Education with the publication of papers on key educational issues.

The participants gathered in the spirit of exploring
the fundamental question of compulsory education. Arguments regarding how the compulsory education institutions should be modified were avoided. The emphasis
was on a reconsideration of compulsion as it relates to
education.

These essays do not resolve the still unanswered questions of compulsory schooling. However, they do focus
the question, perhaps as well as it has ever been focused.
One participant, E. G. West, commented that to the best
of his knowledge "the last time that such thorough ex-
ploration occurred was in mid-nineteenth century England."

The whole subject, clearly, is ripe for rethinking. Not
only has the criticism of compulsory schooling reached a
new high, but also the movement to create alternatives
to the present system is gathering new force. Fundamental issues that have lain dormant for a century are sur-
facing explosively. There could not be a better time to

issue this thought-provoking discussion of the fundamental question of modern mass schooling—the use of governmental compulsion.

SPONSORS AND CONTRIBUTORS

The Center for Independent Education, co-sponsor, encourages educational environment independent of governmental control. Convinced of the value of independence in education, its founders established the center to assist those who study concepts and principles related to education in a free society.

A survey conducted in 1968 by the Center for Independent Education revealed that headmasters overwhelmingly agreed on the increasing difficulties in meeting operating expenses, raising funds for capital improvements and attracting students whose parents could afford the rising tuitions while still paying the mounting public school taxes. Through research, seminars, publications, conferences and other activities, the center exists to support headmasters, trustees, teachers and others concerned with meeting the challenges of freedom of choice for education.

> Address: Center for Independent Education
> P. O. Box 2256
> Wichita, Kansas 67201

The Institute for Humane Studies, co-sponsor, was founded in 1961 as an independent center to encourage basic research and advanced study for the strengthening of a free society. Through conferences, fellowships, publications, and other activities, the institute seeks to serve scholars in all the humane sciences who are interested in extending the knowledge and practice of the principles of liberty. Individuals and organizations in education, business, and the professions throughout the world share in its work and participate in the programs it sponsors or helps others to arrange.

  Address: Institute For Humane Studies, Inc.
           1134 Crane Street
           Menlo Park, California 94025

ROBERT P. BAKER holds a doctorate in jurisprudence from Seton Hall University although his undergraduate work at New York University and Rutgers was in the physical sciences and he was for many years a professional research scientist before turning to the law. A native and disaffected New Yorker, he is now engaged in private law practice in rural southwestern Missouri. As a free-lance author he has published in many different fields. He is widely known for his work in various aspects of compulsory education. See in particular his "Compulsory Education in the United States: Big Brother Goes to School," *Seton Hall Law Review,* Vol. 3, No. 2 (Spring, 1972); "An Approach to Libertarian Jurisprudence," *Libertarian Handbook* (1972); *The Libertarian Philosophy: An Introduction* (pamphlet, New York Libertarian Association: New York, 1971).

H. GEORGE RESCH received his A.B. from Lawrence College in 1960. From 1960 to 1962 he served as researcher and then liaison officer with the William Volker Fund. During 1962 and 1963 he did graduate work in American history at Indiana University. From 1964 to 1970 he served as sales representative for an educational printing house in Chicago. Since 1970 he has been research fellow at the Institute for Humane Studies, specializing in the study of education in a free society, and in the theory and measurement of human individuality and differentiation.

MURRAY N. ROTHBARD is professor of economics, Polytechnic Institute of Brooklyn, and associate, University Seminar on the History of Legal and Political Thought, Columbia University. He is a member of the Council of Advisers, Institute for Humane Studies; Executive Committee, National Taxpayers Union; chairman, Board of Academic Advisers, Society for Individual Liberty; Board of Advisers, National Committee to Legalize Gold. Among his publications are *Man, Economy and State* (Van Nostrand, 1962); *America's Great Depression* (Van Nostrand, 1963); *The Panic of 1819* (Columbia University Press, 1962); *Power and Market* (Institute for Humane Studies, 1970); *For A New Liberty* (Macmillan, 1973). "Plus," says he, "numerous other articles contributed to books, and in magazines, ranging from professional journals to magazines of opinion, left, right, and center."

JOEL HENRY SPRING received his doctorate in education from the University of Wisconsin and is associate professor of education, Case Western University (Cleveland, Ohio). He is author of *Education and the Rise of the Corporate State* (Beacon Press, 1972) and co-author (with Edgar Gumbert) of *American Education in the Twentieth Century* (John Wiley, 1972) and (with Clarence Karier and Paul Violas) of *Roots of Crisis* (Rand McNally, 1972). His articles have appeared in *History of Education Quarterly, School and Society, School Review, Libertarian Analysis, Educational Theory*, and *Socialist Revolution*.

E. G. WEST was graduated in economics from Exeter University (England) in 1948. In 1962 he was appointed lecturer in economics at the University of Newcastle upon Tyne. After a year as a research fellow at the University of Chicago (1965) he became reader in economics at the University of Kent (1966 - 1970). He is now professor of economics at Carleton University, Ottawa. He is author of *Education and the State* (1965) and *Adam Smith: The Man and His Works* (1969). His newest work, *Education and Industrial Revolution*, will be published by Batsford's, London, 1974. His articles have appeared in *Journal of Political Economy, Southern Economic Journal, Philosophy, Economica, Journal of Law and Economics, Economic History Review*, and *Kyklos.*

GERRIT H. WORMHOUDT received his L.L.B. from Northwestern University in 1952 and is an attorney in private practice in Wichita, Kansas. He specializes in labor law, civil rights, and corporate trial work. He is a member of the Kansas bar and the American Bar Association; is admitted to practice before the U. S. Supreme Court; and has tried (and won) cases before the Supreme Court. He is a trustee of the Wichita Collegiate School, a model alternative to compulsory government-financed schooling.

* * *

We begin with a comprehensive history of compulsory education, so that we may understand how we arrived at our current status. Professor Rothbard, a noted libertarian economist and historian, pays particular attention to the dubious rationales used in England and the United States to justify laws compelling parents to send their children to school.

Historical Origins

Murray N. Rothbard

Compulsory schooling began, in the modern world, with the Protestant Reformation. Before the Reformation, instruction had been carried out privately—in church schools and universities, in private schools, and in private guild schools for occupational training. But Martin Luther, in his famous letter to the German rulers in 1524, urged the establishment of public schools, and compulsory attendance, and did so on the basis of a military analogy:

> Dear rulers...I maintain that the civil authorities are un-
> der obligation to compel the people to send their children
> to school....If the government can compel such citizens
> as are fit for military service to bear spear and rifle, to
> mount ramparts, and perform other material duties in
> time of war, how much more has it a right to compel the
> people to send their children to school, because in this
> case we are warring with the devil, whose object it is secret-
> ly to exhaust our cities and principalities of their strong
> men.[1]

Influenced by Luther, the German state of Gotha
founded the first modern public schools in 1524, and
Thuringia followed suit in 1527. Luther himself devised
the Saxony School Plan, which was established in Saxony
in 1528 through an edict drawn up by Luther's disciple
Melanchthon, and which set up public schools in every
town in the region. The first compulsory attendance system was established, again under Lutheran influence, by
the duke of Württemberg in 1559; attendance was compulsory, detailed records were kept, and fines were levied on truants. The Saxon and Württemberg systems
formed the basis for compulsory public schools in most
of the Protestant German states, and later in Prussia.
The major purpose of the school system was theocratic:
to use the power of the government to compel adher-
ence to Lutheranism, and to aid in the suppression of
dissent from the established church. An English admirer
of the Prussian school system writes of Luther's achievement:

> The permanent and positive value of Luther's pronounce-
> ment of 1524 lies not so much in its direct effects as in
> the hallowed associations which it established for Protes-
> tant Germany between the national religion and the edu-
> cational duties of the individual and the state. Thus,
> doubtless, was created that healthy public opinion which
> rendered the principle of compulsory school attendance

easy of acceptance in Prussia at a much earlier date than in England.[2]

The other leading influence on the establishment of compulsory schooling in the modern world—and one even more relevant to the United States—was that other great reformer, John Calvin. Once again, the major object for public schools was to inculcate obedience to a Calvinist-run government, and thereby to aid in the suppression of dissent. As ruler of Geneva in the mid-sixteenth century, Calvin established a number of compulsory public schools in the city, and under his influence Calvinist Holland established compulsory public schools in the early seventeenth century.

It is hardly a coincidence, then, that compulsory and public schooling appeared first in America under the aegis of the Calvinist Puritans, particularly in the leading Puritan colony of Massachusetts Bay. While voluntary parental education, and largely private education, prevailed outside of New England, the militant Puritans who founded the Massachusetts Bay Colony were eager to adopt the Calvinist plan for compulsory education in order to ensure the perpetuation of Calvinism and the suppression of possible dissent. Only a year after passing its first set of laws, the colony, in 1642, enacted a compulsory literacy law for all children; furthermore, the law provided that should state officials judge parents to be unfit or unable to care for their children properly, the government would then seize the children and "apprentice" them to itself to impart the required instruction. Five years later the colony followed up this law with the establishment of a system of public schools.

Puritan influence spread swiftly from Massachusetts to the other colonies of New England, and compulsory schooling spread to the same degree. High Puritan Connecticut soon imposed compulsory schools, and, in 1742, that colony attempted to suppress the dissenting "New Light" movement by prohibiting that sect from operating any schools. Connecticut gave the reason that, if permitted to operate schools, the New Light sect "may tend to train youth in ill principles and practices, and introduce such disorders as may be of fatal consequence to the public peace and weal of this colony."[3] For its part, the more tolerant Pilgrim colony of Plymouth did not establish a compulsory school system until it merged into Massachusetts Bay. It is no coincidence that the one New England colony that did not establish a public school system was Rhode Island, which was founded and peopled by heretics from Calvinist orthodoxy.)

After the founding of the American Republic, Massachusetts, again followed by the remainder of New England, pioneered in establishing public schools and compulsory attendance legislation.)In its constitution of 1780, Massachusetts expressly granted authority to the legislature to enforce compulsory attendance at school. Accordingly, in 1789, Massachusetts enacted the first general school law in the country, mandating public schools throughout the state, certifying school teachers, specifying curricula, and enforcing compulsory attendance at school. Vermont, New Hampshire, and Connecticut rapidly followed suit (Maine at that time adopted the system as a district of Massachusetts), with only Rhode Island again refusing to join the rest of New England.[4]

One of the most enthusiastic supporters of a public and compulsory school system was the "Essex Junto," a group of prominent Federalist merchants and lawyers in Boston hailing originally from Essex County, Massachusetts. The Essexmen were particularly eager for an ex-

tensive public school system so as to have the youth
("taught proper subordination.)' For, as Essexman Stephen Higginson, a leading Boston merchant, put it,("the
people must be *taught* to confide in and reverence their
rulers.") A particularly important theoretician for the Essex Junto was Jonathan Jackson, also a prominent Boston merchant, who set forth his systematic social views in
his *Thoughts Upon the Political Situation of the United
States* (1788). Jackson yearned for the colonial era, with
its "habits of subordination" to a government of the
elite, in which Jackson and his colleagues believed that all
political power should be lodged. Jackson and the other
Essexmen held that society was "one large family," in
which "father" (the elite) should firmly rule, thus forming a "perfect whole" in which each man should be
"learning his proper place and keeping to it." Historian
David Hackett Fischer justly refers to Jackson and the
other Essexmen as "collectivists," who "had no fear of an
enlarged economic role for government, as long as it
was administered by the natural leaders of society. They
favored bounties, tariffs, rebates, drawbacks, licenses,
subsidies, and also prohibitions, inspections, and all
manner of restrictions."[5] It is no wonder, then, that
Jackson, expressing the Essexmen's enthusiastic support
for public and compulsory schooling, had the courage to
pursue the logic to that other important medium of education, the newspaper press. Jackson denounced the pri-
vately-owned press for being necessarily dependent on
its readership, and advocated a government-owned
newspaper that could be independent of its readers and
could therefore inculcate the proper virtues in the citizens.

In the new nation the idea arose early that compulsory schooling was mandatory because the children be-

longed to the government and not to their parents.
Thus, as early as 1785, the Reverend Jeremy Belknap of
New Hampshire advocated equal and compulsory
schooling for all, emphasizing that the children belong
to the government rather than to their parents.[6] The
doctrine of obedience to the government was also the
major theme of the founder of the public school system
in North Carolina, the judge and financier Archibald
Douglas Murphey. In 1816 Murphey outlined a system
of public schools as follows:

> ...all the children shall be taught in them...in these
> schools the precepts of morality and religion should be
> inculcated, and habits of subordination and obedience be
> formed....Their parents know not how to instruct
> them....The state, in the warmth of her affection and so-
> licitude for their welfare must take charge of those chil-
> dren and place them in school where their minds can be
> enlightened and their hearts can be trained to virtue.[7]

Compulsion can be used to consolidate the rule of a
governing class or to impose an unnatural equality and
uniformity upon the subjects. To the socialists and educational reformers Frances Wright and Robert Dale Ow-
en, compulsory uniformity was the goal of their
proposals for total governmental control of the schools.
Their scheme was "national, rational, republican education; free for all at the expense of all, conducted under
the guardianship of the state, and for the honor, the
happiness, the virtue, the salvation of the state." But to
accomplish this task, and to impose equality on all the
children, the public schools must have the children
twenty-four hours a day, year-round, from the age of
two to sixteen. Owen summarized the plan:

> The system of public education, then, which we consider
> capable, and only capable, of regenerating this nation,

and of establishing practical virtue and republican equality among us, is one which provides for all children at all
times; receiving them at the earliest age...feeding, clothing and educating them, until the age of majority.

We propose that all the children so adopted should receive the same food; should be dressed in the same simple clothing; should experience the same kind treatment;
should be taught (until their professional education com-
mences) in the same branches; in a word, that nothing sa-
voring of inequality, nothing reminding them of the pride
of riches or the contempt of poverty, should be suffered
to enter these republican safeguards of a young nation of
equals.[8]

In this way, Wright and Owen hoped that the entire society would be rendered equal, and the nation would be
ripe for the final step—the equalization of property and
incomes by governmental coercion.

While the Wright-Owen plan was never put into full
force, serious attention was paid to the proposal by contemporary educationists. Many prominent newspapers
supported the scheme, and the widely noted report on
education by a committee of Philadelphia workingmen
in 1829 was studded with citations and theory from the
works of Owen and Wright; this report, in turn, was influential in the spread of public and compulsory schooling during the 1830s.

The earliest opposition to the idea of compulsory
equality came from the workingmen's groups, especially
in New York, where the Workingmen's Party rejected
the scheme. The labor historian Herbert Harris writes
despairingly of their attitude:

In short, labor as a whole didn't want anything basically
new or different; it wanted to share more fully in the advantages of existing commercial and industrial arrangements. It wanted for itself what the "haves" possessed. It
wanted its children to rise in the world.[9]

By the middle of the nineteenth century America had its first group of professional educationists. The principal figures in this close though informal body of professionals were a group led by Horace Mann of Massachusetts and including Henry Barnard of Connecticut, James G. Carter of Massachusetts, Caleb Mills of Indiana, and Samuel Lewis and Calvin Stowe of Ohio. The tireless efforts of these few men were instrumental in expanding the public school system, in establishing a compulsory system, and in gaining for themselves positions of power in its structure. One method used to achieve their goals was to establish a welter of interlocking educational organizations. One of the first was the American Lyceum, organized in 1826 by Josiah Holbrook to influence and dominate state and local boards of education. In 1827 the first Society for the Promotion of Public Schools was organized in Pennsylvania to engage in an extensive program of correspondence, pamphleteering, and press releases. Similar societies were formed in the early 1830s, featuring lectures, meetings, and legislative lobbying. Hundreds of such associations arose throughout the country, like the American Institute of Instruction, founded in New England in 1830. The annual meetings and papers of this institute served as a clearing house and discussion center for the educationist movement.

Furthermore, the educationists published journals by the dozens, through which their theories and arguments were disseminated to their followers. The leading publications were the *American Journal of Education*, and its successor, the *American Annals of Education*, the *Common School Assistant* (J. Orville Taylor, editor), the *Connecticut Common School Journal* (Henry Barnard, editor), and the *Common School Journal* (Horace Mann, editor).

The most important single channel of educationist influence ran through high positions in the public school
systems. Thus, Horace Mann, editor of the *Common
School Journal*, became the first secretary of the Massachusetts Board of Education, and his annual reports
during the 1840s served to promote the educationists'
"line." Henry Barnard became secretary of the Connecticut Board of Education, Calvin Wiley became head of
the public schools in North Carolina, Caleb Mills in Indiana, Samuel Lewis in Ohio, and so on.

Another institution where the educationists came into
positions of power and domination was the teacher
training college, from which future teachers would
emerge. As a corollary, educationists came to determine
the standards for the certification of teachers. Thus,
through their combined efforts they succeeded in establishing effective control over the nation's corps of public
school teachers.

The educationists generally did not go so far as to advocate compulsory schooling openly, but they did everything up to that point by calling upon everyone to
attend public schools and by consistently disparaging
private schools. They were eager for universal public
school attendance in order to hasten the equality of children, and, bye the bye, to magnify their own power and
income. The influence of Wright-Owen concepts was
evident in their stress on equality and uniformity. Thus,
Samuel Lewis emphasized that the common schools were
to take a diverse population and mould them into "one
people." Theodore Edson exulted that in the common
schools the good children must learn to mingle with the
bad ones, as they supposedly would have to do in later
life. The influential J. Orville Taylor wrote in his *Common School Assistant* in 1837, echoing the sentiments of
Wright and Owen, "let the common school *be made fit*

to educate all, and let all send to it" (italics his). Taylor
then hailed the "spirit of common schools. . . . Where the
rich and the poor meet together on equal terms, where
high and low are taught in the same house, the same
class, and out of the same book, and by the same teacher. . .this is a republican education."[10]

In fact, the Virginia Federalist and educationist
Charles Fenton Mercer delivered a speech in 1826 anticipating the Wright-Owen drive for compulsory equality
via the public school. Mercer declared:

> . . .the equality on which our institutions are founded
> cannot be too intimately interwoven in the habits of think-
> ing among our youth; and it is obvious that it would be
> greatly promoted by their continuance together, for the
> longest possible period, in the same schools of juvenile in-
> struction; to sit upon the same forms; engage in the same
> competitions; partake of the same recreations and amuse-
> ments, and pursue the same studies, in connection with
> each other; under the same discipline, and in obedience
> to the same authority.[11]

Hand in hand with such sentiments went disparage-
ment of the private schools. This theme appeared almost universally in the educationist writings. James G.
Carter stressed the point in the 1820s; and Orville Taylor attacked private schools in terms reminiscent of Ow-
en, charging that if a rich child is sent to a private
school, he will be taught "to look upon certain classes as
inferior, and born to fewer privileges. This is not republican."[12]

Part of the task of compulsory uniformity that the educationists sought as early as the mid-nineteenth century
was to tame, mould, and assimilate the troubling influx
of immigrants, at first particularly Irish Catholics, who
came pouring into the New World. Educationist Benja-

min Labaree, president of Middlebury College, address-
ing the influential American Institute of Instruction, in
1849, worried about the "multitude of emigrants from
the old world, interfused among our population" who
were "rapidly changing the identity of American character." The problem was that "these strangers among us,
ignorant of our institutions" might well come to "mistake
lawless freedom from restraint, for true and rational liberty." Whether these immigrants shall "become a part of
the body politic" or whether they "will prove to our republic what the Goths and Huns were to the Roman
Empire," depends in large part "upon the wisdom and
fidelity of our teachers." In short, Labaree saw the task
of the schoolteacher as the inculcation of American values into the mass of immigrants, and so "by degrees [to]
mould these unprepared and uncongenial elements into
the form and character which the peculiar nature of the
[American] edifice demands...."[13]

A vital part of this inculcation and moulding, for Labaree and the other educationists, was what they re-
ferred to as "Christianizing" the immigrants—in the case
of the Irish Catholics, of course, a euphemism for Prot-
estantizing. George B. Cheever, in 1854, put the thesis
more bluntly. He declared that "we are in great danger
from the dark and stolid infidelity and vicious radicalism
of a large portion of the foreign immigrating population." The remedy was the public school:

> ...how can we reach the evil at its roots, applying a wise
> and conservative radicalism to defeat the working of that
> malignant, social, anti-Christian poison? How can the chil-
> dren of such a population be reached, except in our free
> public schools?[14]

And so the educationists of the mid-nineteenth century saw themselves as using an expanded network of

free public schools to shape and render uniform all American citizens, to unify the nation, to assimilate the foreigner, to stamp all citizens as Americans, and to impose cohesion and stability on the often unruly and diverse aspirations of the disparate individuals who make up the country.[15] A part of this compulsory cohesion was the imposing of national values on the sometimes unruly lower classes. Horace Mann (a paradigm of what would now be called a "corporate liberal") was anxious to use the public schools to drive out of the lower classes any thought of violence or rebellion, in which he included not only such actual rebellions of the 1840s as the anti-rent war in New York and the Dorr Rebellion in Rhode Island, but also Jacksonian "mobocracy." In his annual report for 1848, Mann wrote:

> Had the obligations of the future citizens been sedulously inculcated upon all the children of the Republic would the patriot have had to mourn over so many instances where the voter, not being able to accomplish his purpose by voting, has proceeded to accomplish it by violence...?[16]

Great care must be taken, Mann added, to "inform and regulate the will of the people."

If the ideal of the educationists was to stamp everyone as American, their cherished system was remarkably Prussian. Calvin Stowe, reporting to the Ohio legislature, hailed the Prussian methods of public education, and urged their adoption in America. Writing in the late 1830s in almost the same terms as Martin Luther, the inspirer of the Prussian system three centuries earlier, Stowe urged that universal compulsory school duty be placed on the same terms as military duty:

> If a regard to the public safety makes it right for a government to compel the citizens to do military duty when

the country is invaded, the same reason authorizes the government to compel them to provide for the education of their children—for no foes are so much to be dreaded as ignorance and vice. A man has no more right to endanger the state by throwing upon it a family of ignorant and vicious children than he has to give admission to the spies of an invading army. If he is unable to educate his children the state should assist him—if unwilling, it should compel him. General education is as much more certain, and much less expensive, than military array . . . .[17]

Other principles that Stowe admired in the Prussian system were its enforcement of a uniform language upon the various nationalities and linguistic groups, and the strongly enforced attendance laws and anti-truant laws. His report on Prussian education was highly influential among the educationists, and the majority followed his lead. Henry Barnard praised the Prussian educational system and urged that "regular attendance at the school shall be an object of special control and the most active vigilance. . . . It would be very fortunate if parents and children were always willing of themselves. Unhappily, this is not the case, particularly in great cities. Although it is lamentable to be forced to use constraint, it is almost always necessary to commence with it."[18]

And, some decades later, educationist Newton Bateman, influenced by Prussian thought, wrote of the government's "right of eminant domain" over the "minds and souls and bodies" of all individuals, including of course the children. Hence, education "cannot be left to the caprices and contingencies of individuals. . . ."[19]

In addition to the more grandiose aims of compulsion, the educationists were also concerned to increase their personal power and pelf. As directors of the educational establishment, they drove systematically to extend their power and to induce or force an ever widening circle of pupils into their schools. As Professor E. G. West points out, the drive of educationists and teachers to make the public schools free succeeded in New York State in 1867. Before that, the public schools had been supported by tuition, and therefore their customers were limited, as in all areas of the economy, by the need to pay for the cost of the service. Hence the drive of these educational suppliers to force the taxpayers to pay for, and thereby expand the demand for, their own services. The argument used before 1867 was that the lack of universal attendance in the public schools was due to the existence of poverty. When attendance still fell short of the universal even after 1867, the educationists changed their argument and denounced parents for being wilful, ignorant, and indifferent to the benefits of the education being offered free to their children. Hence the need for the coercive device of compulsory attendance, which the educationists were able to drive through the New York legislature in 1874.[20]

By the end of the nineteenth century, the educationists had built a public school system that came under increasing criticism for its heavy bureaucracy, its system of crippling rules, and its insistence on uniformity, regularity and conformity with these universal rules. Curricula and teaching methods were increasingly standardized, thus ignoring the enormous differences between groups and individuals.[21]

We now begin to see why it should not be a source of wonder that the poorer people and the working classes were the major opponents of the new public school program. Michael Katz, writing about the successful struggle in 1860, in Beverly, Massachusetts, to abolish the public high school, points out that the wealthy groups were almost unanimously in favor of keeping the public high school while the working classes and poorer groups—the farmers, shoemakers, mariners, fishermen, and laborers—were almost unanimously in favor of its abolition.[22]

By the turn of the twentieth century, the public school system had achieved its maximum impact throughout the country; compulsory attendance laws, furthermore, had swept through state after state, and by 1918 every state in the recalcitrant South had been conquered by the system of compulsion. The public school system was ready for its next transformation, for the consolidation of its dominance and for the intensification of its control by a ruling elite. During the first decades of the century, the Progressive era brought a rapid and fateful shift from a roughly laissez-faire economy and society toward the general structure of a corporate society in America, dominated by an alliance of government, important segments of business, and newly developing labor unions as a junior partner. In recent years, historians, led by Samuel P. Hays and James Weinstein, have begun to show the corollary impact of the Progressive movement on the workings of municipal government.[23]

The Progressive period was marked by a conscious shift of urban political power from local neighborhoods and wards, representing the mass of lower-income and middle-income citizens, toward a centralized rule by upper-income and business groups. The shift was cleverly put forward as the ouster of "corrupt" political party bosses and "ward heelers" on behalf of efficient, "nonpartisan" technicians, invariably consisting of upper-income and business groups. It became important for upper-income groups to control municipal governments as the scope of government intervention and activity accelerated, and as governments increasingly became the coveted source of contracts, franchises, tax assessments, and subsidies.

The city manager and city commission movements were particular examples of the concentration of urban power in the hands of a small upper-class elite. Part of this shift of power away from a decentralized, ward and neighborhood representation included a shift of control of the local school boards as well. Each school board had originally been controlled by its urban ward (by its "community"), and the Progressive impact on municipal affairs involved the centralization of urban school systems into single, overall school boards dominated by upper-class citizens.[24]

An example is the city of Pittsburgh. In pre-reform Pittsburgh, in 1910, of the 387 members of local ward-elected school boards and the city council, one-quarter were upper-class managers, professionals, bankers, and big businessmen; while two-thirds were small businessmen and white-collar workers and laborers. The two leading reform organizations were the Civic Club and the Voters' League, two-thirds of whom were upper-class members, and all of whom were professionals or big businessmen and their wives. The Voters' League stated explicitly that a major aim of reform was to replace lower-class people on the school boards by "men prominent throughout the city . . . ."[25] The reformers did not succeed within the city; but they won by making an end run around the city itself. In 1911, the Pennsylvania legislature went over the heads of the city and imposed a new city charter and a new school board system upon Pittsburgh. To make sure that all would be well, the governor appointed all the members of the new, small centralized city council, and the judges of the state court of common pleas appointed all the members of the new city-wide school board. Of the new nine-man city council (replacing the 36-man council in the old system), six were upper-class big businessmen and two were upper-class physicians (the ninth man was a union official); of the new fifteen-man city school board, none was a small businessman or worker; instead, ten were big businessmen, three were upper-class wives, one an upper-class physician, and one a union official. The upper-class centralizers had won in Pittsburgh, much to the chagrin of the lower and middle classes in the city.[26]

The educationist and educational historian Elwood P. Cubberley put the case for urban school centralization in a forthright manner:

> One of the important results of the change from ward representation to election from the city at large...is that the inevitable representation from these "poor wards" is eliminated, and the board comes to partake of the best characteristics of the city as a whole.

Otherwise, he warned, the "less intelligent and progressive element would wear out the better elements and come to rule the board." Who were these "better elements"? Cubberley answers clearly:

> Men who are successful in the handling of large business undertakings—manufacturers, merchants, bankers, contractors, and professional men of large practice—would perhaps come first....[27]

Once again, one of the leading reasons for tightening central control of the public schools was the troublesome wave of immigration in the late nineteenth and early twentieth centuries; more than ever it was important to the educationists to direct, assimilate, and control the new immigrants, and to mould them into the older and more homogeneous system. Immigrants were expected to abandon their previous language, as well as their often contrasting and diverse values and cultures. In some cases, evening schools were compulsory for non-English-speaking immigrants; but of course the public school undertook the major part of the work. It was not an easy task; immigrants often clung to their own culture, and the pesky Catholics often insisted on establishing their own parochial schools.

Quantitatively, the educationists have achieved a success in the twentieth century beyond their fondest expectations. An increasingly large proportion of Americans have been induced or dragooned into grammar school, high school, college, and now even graduate school. This development has been aided by steady rises in the minimum school-leaving age, as well as by massive governmental grants and subsidies to higher education, much of which is now government-operated. Qualitatively, the success story of the educationists is open to question. But one quantitative attempt—the final and logical culmination of the educationists' dream of universal and compulsory public schooling—was to prove abortive. On November 7, 1922, the state of Oregon, unhappy with allowing the existence of private schools even when government-certified, passed a law prohibiting all private schools and compelling all children to attend public school. It was indeed the fulfilment of the dreams of the educationists; at last all private schools were to be stamped out, and all children were to be subjected to the universal "democratizing," the great cohesion, of the public school.

It is instructive to note who the major forces were in the drive to outlaw the private school. It was not led, at least directly, by the Progressive educators, by the local reincarnations of Henry Barnard or Horace Mann. On the contrary, the spearhead of the drive for the law was the Ku Klux Klan, then strong in the northern states; for the Klan was eager to crush the Catholic parochial school system, and to force all Catholic and immigrant children into the neo-Protestantizing and "Americanizing" force of the public school. The Klan, it is interesting to note, declared that such a law was necessary for the "preservation of free institutions." And if we ponder the history of compulsory education in America, it may well seem that the Klan and the "liberal" educational reformers were not so far apart after all.[28]

Fortunately, the Oregon law was struck down by the Supreme Court in 1925 (*Pierce v. Society of Sisters*, June 1, 1925). The court declared that "the child is not the mere creature of the state," and vigorously asserted that the Oregon law clashed with "the fundamental theory of liberty upon which all governments in this Union repose." Whether all governments in this Union do indeed repose on libertarian theory is another issue; but the *Pierce* decision points the way to a fundamental choice that must eventually be made with respect to public and compulsory schooling in America: either *Pierce* and liberty or Horace Mann and the Ku Klux Klan.

NOTES

[1]John William Perrin, *The History of Compulsory Education in New England* (Meadville, Pa., 1896).

[2]A. E. Twentyman, "Education: Germany," *Encyclopedia Britannica* (14th ed.,) Vol. 7, pp. 999-1000.

[3]Merle Curti, *The Social Ideas of American Educators* (Totowa, N.J.: Littlefield, Adams, 1966), p. 10.

[4]Lawrence Cremin, *The American Common School: An Historic Conception* (New York: Teachers College, Columbia University, 1951), p. 87.

[5]David Hackett Fischer, "The Myth of the Essex Junto," *William and Mary Quarterly* (April, 1964), pp. 191-235. Also see Murray N. Rothbard, "Economic Thought: Comment," in D.T. Gilchrist, ed., *The Growth of the Seaport Cities, 1790-1825* (Charlottesville, Va.: University Press of Virginia, 1967), pp. 178-79.

[6]Hans Kohn, *The Idea of Nationalism* (New York, 1934), p. 104.

[7]*The Papers of Archibald D. Murphey* (Raleigh, N.C.: Hazzell, 1914), II, pp. 53-54.

[8]Cremin, *op. cit.*, p. 41. See also Joseph Dorfman, *The Economic Mind in American Civilization, 1606-1865* (New York: Viking Press, 1946) II, p. 642 ff.

[9]Herbert Harris, *American Labor* (New Haven: Yale University Press, 1939), pp. 26-27. Quoted in Cremin, *op. cit.*, p. 42.

[10]Cremin, *op. cit.*, p. 59.

[11]Charles Fenton Mercer, *A Discourse on Popular Education* (Princeton, 1826), p. 76. Quoted in Cremin, *op. cit.*, p. 57.

[12]Cremin, *op. cit.*, p. 60.

[13]*Ibid.*, pp. 45-46.

[14]*Ibid.*, pp. 46-47.

[15]Cf. Robert H. Wiebe, "The Social Functions of Public Education," *American Quarterly* (Summer, 1969), p. 148.

[16]Horace Mann, Report for 1848, *Life and Works* (Boston: Lee and Shepard, 1891), III, p. 696. Quoted in Curti, *op. cit.*, p. 129.

[17]Calvin E. Stowe, *The Prussian System of Public Instruction and Its Applicability to the United States* (Cincinnati: Truman and Smith, 1836).

[18]Henry Barnard, *National Education in Europe* (Hartford, Conn.: Case, Tiffany & Co., 1854).

[19]Quoted in Edward Chase Kirkland, *Dream and Thought in the Business Community, 1860-1900* (Chicago: Quadrangle Books, 1964), p. 54.

[20]E. G. West, "The Political Economy of American Public School Legislation," *Journal of Law and Economics* (October, 1967), pp. 124-27.

[21]See David Tyack, "Bureaucracy and the Common School: The Example of Portland, Oregon, 1851-1913," *American Quarterly* (Fall, 1967), pp. 476-77.

[22]Michael B. Katz, *The Irony of Early School Reform* (Cambridge: Harvard University Press, 1968).

[23]See Samuel P. Hays, "The Politics of Reform in Municipal Government in the Progressive Era," *Pacific Northwest Quarterly* (October, 1964), reprinted in B. Bernstein and A. Matusow, eds., *Twentieth-Century America: Recent Interpretations* (New York: Harcourt, Brace, and World, 1969), pp. 34-58; and James Weinstein, *The Corporate Ideal in the Liberal State, 1900-1916* (Boston: Beacon Press, 1968), pp. 92-116. Also see Milton Kotler, *Neighborhood Government* (Indianapolis: Bobbs Merrill, 1969).

[24]In addition to Hays and Weinstein, *op. cit.*, see David K. Cohen and Marvin Lazerson, "Education and the Corporate Order," *Socialist Revolution* (March-April 1972), p. 66.

[25]Hays, *op. cit.*, pp. 43, 45.

[26]*Ibid.*, pp. 49-50.

[27]Elwood P. Cubberley, *Public School Administration* (Cambridge: Harvard University Press, 1916), pp. 93, 124-25; quoted in Cohen and Lazerson, *op. cit.*, pp. 66-67.

[28]See Lloyd P. Jorgenson, "The Oregon School Law of 1922: Passage and Sequel," *Catholic Historical Review* (October 1968), pp. 455-66. Also see David B. Tyack, "The Perils of Pluralism: The Background of The Pierce Case," *American History Review* (October 1968), pp. 74-98.

The incredible diversity of the human being is explored here by George Resch. The biological, environmental, cultural and religious differences among us are so vast, he suggests, that they pose special difficulties for standardized democratic public education. Mr. Resch's paper points toward the need for a free, pluralistic school system in a pluralistic culture, as the best way to guarantee maximum opportunity for each child.

Human Variation and Individuality

H. George Resch

Compulsory schooling is championed in the United States on a number of grounds. Of the reasons usually offered in defense of this policy, the most common seems to be that only by such means will we be able to achieve equality—or equality of opportunity. Our purpose in this paper will be to explore briefly such questions as: "Are individual human beings equal or do they differ in significant ways? Can they be made equal, or at least guaranteed equality of opportunity? Can these goals be reached with the aid of compulsory schooling?

What effect does compulsory schooling have?"

"We hold these truths to be self-evident . . . that all men are created equal. . . ." It is hard to imagine that Thomas Jefferson when writing the American Declaration of Independence had any idea of the far-ranging effect these words would have. Is Jefferson's statement true or is it what Plato called a "noble lie"—a statement, false in fact, but which will, one hopes, lead to beneficial results if generally accepted? Or, how accurate is the statement found in the Encyclopaedia of the Social Sciences that "at birth human infants, regardless of their heredity, are as equal as Fords"?[1]

The first difficulty in approaching the idea of equality is to learn what is meant by the term. This difficulty has been recognized even by many of equality's most ardent champions. Two American authors of a study advocating a closer approach to equality, while calling it a key value on which everyone ought to agree, admit that "unfortunately general equality is almost impossible to define."[2] Similarly, in commenting on this difficulty, Professor Daniel J. Boorstin wrote:

> Take our concept of equality, which many have called the central American value. No sooner does one describe a subject like this and try to separate it for study, than one finds it diffusing and evaporating into the general atmosphere. "Equality," what does it mean? In the United States it has been taken for a fact and an ideal, a moral imperative and a sociological datum, a legal principle and a social norm.[3]

Despite its lack of a precise and accepted meaning, this word "equality" continues to be used as an incantation, the mere utterance of which is expected to command assent. As one commentator declared:

> Equality is a charmed term. It fascinates reformers.

Prophets that wait for signs and portents are almost unanimous in predictions of a widening social equality. When the word can no longer be used indiscriminately, it is still retained as defining an indispensable principle of progress. This and that necessary qualification may be granted; it may be smitten on either cheek with staggering blows, but it is sure to come up sanguine and smiling. It has a charmed life. If it is pushed out the door it comes back through the window. Almost every social theory gets it in somewhere, as a fundamental condition of human welfare. . . . Even when the difficulty in achieving it is recognized, the conviction remains strong that it is desirable, and that effort should constantly be directed toward gaining the little or the much that is attainable—the more the better,—as though there could be no question in a sane mind that inequality is in itself a source of evil.[4]

The difficulty of pinning down a precise meaning that doesn't fly in the face of reality is hardly surprising. For when we survey the entire animate world, we find nothing remotely resembling equality. On the contrary, one of the most important facts of natural science is the all-pervasive variation to be found in nature. We find this to be the case among plants and animals, but probably such variation reaches its apex in man. Each individual, despite certain apparent similarities, differs from his fellow men in myriad ways. It is well known, for example, that each person bears a unique fingerprint design by which he may be distinguished from millions of his fellow men, and in recent years the work of the renowned biochemist Dr. Roger J. Williams has increasingly shown that similar variations between individuals are to be found throughout the body. Considering the incredible range in size or capacity of bodily organs that is nevertheless considered normal, Dr. Williams stresses that:

Normal individuals are highly distinctive with respect to their stomachs, esophagi, hearts, blood vessels, bloods, thoracic ducts, livers, pelvic colons, sinuses, breathing patterns, muscles and their system of endocrine glands. In all these cases inborn differences are observed which are often far beyond what we see externally.[5]

This variation is found in perhaps the most marked degree in the human brain. The late Dr. K. S. Lashley, for years the premier researcher in the area of the brain and nerve functions, summarized the status of our knowledge of inheritance and variation of structure in the central nervous system as follows:

The brain is extremely variable in every character that has been subjected to measurement. Its diversities of structure within the species are of the same general character as are the differences between related species or even orders of animals . . . . Discussions of heredity and environment have tended to regard the nervous system, if it is considered at all, as a vaguely remote organ, essentially similar in all individuals and largely molded by experience. Even the limited evidence at hand, however, shows that individuals start life with brains differing enormously in structure; unlike in number, size, and arrangement of neurons as well as in grosser features. The variations in cells and tracts must have functional significance. It is not conceivable that the inferior frontal convolutions of two brains would function in the same way or with equal effectiveness when one contains only half as many cells as the other; that two parietal association areas should be identical in function when the cells of one are mostly minute granules and of the other large pyramids; that the presence of Betz cells in the prefrontal region is without influence on behavior. Such differences are the rule in the limited material that we have studied.[6]

This information leads Professor Williams to conclude that:

. . . different human brains are as unlike each other as are the brains of different species and even different orders of animals...your brain probably differs from your neighbor's far more than your facial features vary from his....the wide differences in brain structure contribute to make us all spotted with respect to the ease with which we grasp various thoughts, concepts and ideas. This is why we may speak of someone's having a "fine legal mind" or of a person's having a "yen for mathematics" or a student's being a "language whiz." Experts agree that every individual tends to have a pattern of mental abilities or potentialities which is distinctive for him or her alone.[7]

A considerable amount of work has been done in this area in recent years by Professor J. P. Guilford. He and his colleagues at the Aptitudes Research Project at the University of Southern California have extended the demonstrations of intellectual factorial abilities to a total of approximately a hundred. We have reason to believe that each of the intellectual abilities is distributed in accordance with a Gaussian curve of normal distribution throughout the population. It is also known that individuals vary greatly in terms of the unique patterns of abilities they possess. Unfortunately, the fact that what we call intelligence is composed of a kind of mosaic of these nearly one hundred separate factors is easily obscured by the assignment of a single numerical value to the "I.Q." Thus, while a given individual might have an extraordinary aptitude in one field he might also be significantly deficient in another.

When men vary so greatly in their physical makeup and in the structure of their intelligence it should hardly be surprising that their behavior patterns vary as well. Biologist Garrett Hardin asks:

How can we reasonably expect Mr. A and Mr. B to act like some median stereotype if the thyroid and sex-hormones in the blood stream of one are 10 times as great as in the other? How can we reasonably expect all men to have the same safe-driving records when, even among men with "normal" vision, some are 42 times as good as others in detecting movement in the periphery of the visual field? Is it reasonable to expect the same "philosophy of life" in two men, when the blood stream of one has 10 times as much of the basic energy releasing enzymes as are present in the blood of the other? And how can we reasonably demand that all children partake of a "normal" diet, when the vitamin B_1 requirement varies at least four-fold, and the vitamin D requirement at least eight-fold?[8]

If Jefferson should have known better in 1776 than to have written that "all men are created equal" there is even less reason for contemporary scholars to fall into the same error.[9] Jefferson might have been expected to observe around him the widespread inequality, but at that time he was without the scientific explanation for that inequality which was provided by the work of Gregor Mendel and his successors. On the basis of Mendelian law we now know that:

. . . every being conceived by sexual recombination is a genetic accident. Every individual being is thus a pioneer, a biological adventure. No one quite like you can exist in your species. Common heredity may provide a common disposition among contemporaries, or a limited likeness between ancestor and descendant. But the strategy of sex denies the prison of identicality. If you were not created equal, you were yet created free....Sexual recombination imposes diversity on living beings. Evaluated by environment, that diversity becomes inequality.[10]

No matter in what area we look, then, we find no evidence of equality among men. We find instead the most all-encompassing diversity and inequality. However much men may in some ways seem alike, we find on further examination that this similarity is illusory. The assertion, then, that "all men are created equal" is simply not so. Each has his own unique physical, mental, emotional, and behavioral makeup. We can readily agree, then, with Dr. von Mises when he says that "some surpass their fellow men in health and vigor, in brains and aptitude, in energy and resolution and are therefore better suited to the pursuit of earthly affairs than the rest of mankind."[11]

This diversity or inequality, far from being a problem to be overcome, is the basis of much of our civilized social order. If all individuals were the same, there would be no division of labor, no trade would take place, and there would seem to be little purpose to any social intercourse. [It is the differences between individuals, not their similarities, which provide us with opportunity for personal growth and for an ever-richer social order] As Dr. Rothbard points out:

> The development of individual variety tends to be both the cause and the effect of the progress of civilization. As civilization progresses, there is increasing opportunity for the greater development of each person's interests, talents, and reasoning in an expanding number of fields, leading to the growth of his human faculties. And from such opportunities comes the advancement of knowledge which in turn enhances his society's civility. Furthermore, it is the variety of individual interests and talents that permits the growth of specialization and division of labor on which civilized society depends.[12]

In view of the all-pervasive variation found in nature, and especially among men's aptitudes, abilities, and characters, what can we conclude about the goal of equality? Our only reasonable conclusion is that it is not only an unrealizable goal but that any serious effort to achieve it could only result in the destruction of civilized society. For "if each individual is unique, how else can he be made 'equal' to others than by destroying most of what is human in him and reducing human society to the mindless uniformity of the ant heap?"[13]

By virtue of both man's variation and his locational diversity, equality not only cannot be achieved but is a *conceptually* impossible goal for man. And if equality is an impossible goal, any attempt to reach it will be futile, for "if equality is an absurd (and therefore *irrational*) goal, then any effort to approach equality is correspondingly absurd. If a goal is pointless, then any attempt to attain it is similarly pointless."[14]

Even when the difficulties and, indeed, the impossibility of social equality become apparent, however, they are seldom sufficient to cause the votaries of equality to abandon their goal. The demand becomes, not equality *per se,* but "equality of opportunity." Unfortunately, as with its parent idea, its champions seldom specify with any precision what they mean by such a concept. When it is defined at all it is usually done in the most metaphorical terms, "another elastic phrase which means little or much, according to the explanation."[15]

Most often equality of opportunity is defined in a very loose fashion as a sense of fair play necessary in playing the "game of life." Thus, R. H. Tawney in his *Equality* says that:

> Rightly interpreted, it means, not only that what are commonly regarded as the prizes of life should be open to all, but that none should be subjected to arbitrary penalties....If the rules of the game give a permanent advantage to some of the players, it does not become fair merely because they are scrupulously observed by all who take part in it. When the contrast between the circumstances of different social strata is so profound as today, the argument—if it deserves to be called an argument— which suggests that the income they receive bears a close relation to their personal qualities is obviously illusory.[16]

And, similarly, Blum and Kalven say that "In terms of the justice of rewards, the point is that no race can be fair unless the contestants start from the same mark."[17]

And Frank Knight, one of the intellectual founders of the "Chicago School" of economics, also "has repeatedly likened social life to a 'game' or a 'contest,' has talked about the 'distribution of prizes,' has mused on what arrangements tend to make the contest 'interesting to participants and spectators,' and has considered the imposition of 'handicaps.' "[18] But here, as with so many analogies, we can be seriously misled when we mistake our theoretical and metaphorical constructs for reality. After all, as Dr. Rothbard has pointed out, "Human life is not some sort of race or game in which each person should start from an identical mark. It is an attempt by each man to be as happy as possible. And each person *could not* begin from the same point, for the world has not just come into being; it is diverse and infinitely varied in its parts."[19]

So long as individuals, largely as a result of their biological inheritances, vary so greatly, equality of opportunity is simply not possible. What equality of opportunity can there be, for example, between two young people, one brilliantly intelligent and in vigorous good health and the other a mental dullard with a sickly constitution? Is it not obvious that they are marked for different roles in life and that what they need is *unequal* opportunities in accord with their unequal endowments?

Even if we were to believe that differences in intelligence and character were the result of differing environments rather than heredity, the difficulties in trying to achieve equal opportunity via equal environments for all would be insurmountable. It seems doubtful that if the full dimensions of such an egalitarian policy were known, many would favor it. Such a policy would "require the abolition of the family since different parents have unequal abilities; it would require the communal rearing of children; the state would have to nationalize all babies and raise them in state nurseries under 'equal' conditions."[20] But even such draconian measures as these are necessarily doomed to failure, because the various doctors, nurses and other state functionaries involved in the rearing of these children in nurseries, themselves have unique personalities and abilities. Just as no equality of hereditary endowment is possible, neither is a truly equal environment.

It is the supposed ability of universal compulsory schooling to bring about a society of ever greater equality that has come to be its *raison d'être*. Only if we take our children at an early age, it is argued, and provide them with an equal opportunity through the common schools can we overcome the legacy of social and economic inequality. Yet there is hardly an area in which egalitarian measures are more certainly doomed to failure than in compulsory schooling.

As we have seen, each child is marked with his own unique personality, with mental and emotional interests and abilities differing from everyone else's. One child may display an extraordinary interest and aptitude in music and yet show no particular promise in a number of other directions. Another child may be highly talented in mathematics and the sciences.

> One child may be most suited, in interests and ability, to an extensive course in one subject at a time; another may require a study schedule covering several courses at once; and so forth. Given the formal, systematic courses of instruction, there is an infinite variety of pace and course combinations most appropriate for each child.[21]

This means, of course, that it is precisely those unique qualities of the child that are being developed rather than those qualities he may have in common with others. It means that to the extent that we gear education to the child's own requirements we have education leading not to equality but to inequality, to a greater and greater human differentiation. Human differences and distinctions are thus not eliminated, but heightened and enhanced. In this, education differs markedly from the spirit of democratic equality which, as Everett Dean Martin points out:

> ...strives to ignore the cultural differences among people. Education intensifies them. The attempt to place everyone on the same mediocre plane, even though it be a level considerably above the lowest, is not education; it is a kind of social work. Education means finding one's own level. Like all progress it is qualitative and differentiating....It brings out distinctions of human worth, places people on the rounds of a ladder, the gradations of which are discernible in the kinds of interests they have, in the quality of their choices, the perplexities they wrestle with and overcome, the tasks and issues they set themselves.[22]

"Ah, yes," the egalitarian may well respond, "what you have said is no doubt true. If we deliberately set out to give everyone a different and unequal education, why, of course we shall end up with highly unequal individuals as a result. We could hardly expect anything else. That is precisely why we want to equalize educational opportunity by schooling all children with a common curriculum in public schools. It is by such a process that we can hope to achieve or at least approach equality."

Even by subjecting all children to the same curriculum, however, we would still be unable to achieve the desired equality. The inborn differences among individuals are too fundamental a part of their natures to be obliterated even by a decade or more of scholastic engineering. Compulsory schooling not only fails to achieve its egalitarian goal, but by subjecting all to the same studies in lockstep fashion effectively denies them any real opportunity at all. The Reverend George Harris points out:

> Actual opportunity, which not only invites but constrains youth to appropriate it, is not and cannot be an equal opportunity for all. Behind fifty desks exactly alike fifty boys and girls are seated to recite a lesson prescribed to all. Could opportunity be more nearly alike for half a hundred youth? But the algebra is not an opportunity for the boy who has no turn for mathematics. He may throw his head at the book and stand dazed before the blackboard; but the science is not for him any more than the presidency of the United States is for a tramp—perhaps not so much. Indeed, the more nearly equal the opportunity outwardly, the more unequal it is really. When the same instruction for the same number of hours a day by the same teachers is provided for fifty boys and girls the majority have almost no opportunity at all. The bright scholars are held back by the rate possible to the average, the dull scholars are unable to keep up with the average, and only the middle section have anything like a fair opportunity. Even average scholars are discouraged because the brighter students accomplish their tasks so easily and never take their books home....the *prime necessity is inequality of opportunity in agreement with inequality of individuals.*[23][Italics supplied]

It is unlikely, then, that compulsory schooling provides any real opportunity for its conscripted subjects at all. Even if we were, however, to assume that some—or even all—were benefited by it, there would still be no reason to believe that this schooling would "necessarily do anything to diminish the inequalities of either economic class or social status distinctions between groups.

Whatever the benefits for the odd individuals, schooling heightens the inequalities as it becomes more efficient in monopolizing the selection of winners and losers."[24] The effort "comes to grief, in short, because individuals do not all have the same ability to make use of their opportunities with equal or comparable success."[25]

Probably the most extensive—and certainly the most expensive—demonstration of the elusiveness and ambiguity of the concept "equality of educational opportunity," and the inefficacy of compulsory schooling to bring about such equality, was provided by the recent Coleman Report. Because of its significance it will be worthwhile to examine the genesis and conclusion of the report in some detail.

The report was undertaken in response to section 402 of the Civil Rights Act of 1964:

> Sec. 402. The Commissioner shall conduct a survey and make a report to the President and the Congress, within two years of the enactment of this title, concerning the lack of availability of equal educational opportunity for individuals by reason of race, color, religion, or national origin in public educational institutions at all levels in the United States, its territories and possessions, and the District of Columbia.

The study was conducted by Professor James S. Coleman of Johns Hopkins University, aided by a fellow academician and five employees of the U.S. Office of Education. The result was the second longest social science research project ever undertaken. The project involved the testing of 570,000 school pupils and some 60,000 teachers. In addition, information about the facilities available in 4,000 schools was gathered in elaborate detail. The published findings filled a massive volume of 737 pages, accompanied by a supplemental appendix of another 548 pages.[26] Its findings, which have been widely reported in both the popular press and in the scholarly journals, have been extremely upsetting to those who have viewed the public schools as the main agency insuring equality of opportunity in the United States. So shattering were the results, in fact, that the study was itself made the subject of a reexamination by a Harvard faculty seminar during the academic year 1966-1967. The results of this seminar were themselves published in a volume of 572 pages—*On Equality of Educational Opportunity.*[27]

Even more interesting than the conclusions which emerged from this study, however, was the way the authors and the U.S. Office of Education viewed the idea of equality of opportunity. On the basis the Civil Rights Act of 1964, which authorized the study, it seems patently evident that the legislative viewpoint was that the denial of equal opportunity was occasioned by the inferior facilities and personnel available to Negro and other "minority" students. This interpretation is supported by the use of the term *availability,* and it is in full harmony with the then prevailing environmentalist concept of equality of opportunity. This interpretation is also shared by Professors Daniel P. Moynihan and Frederick Mosteller who write:

> Initially Congress seems to have intended the study to become a tool for legal actions opposing formal discrimination against minority groups. As it became evident that the statute would forbid outright any such discriminatory acts, the final attempt may have been to establish once and for all that gross differences in school facilities did exist, especially as between black and white children in the United States. At all events, the statute implied that there was "lack of availability of equal educational opportunities" and the Office of Education set out to document it.[28]

The authors place this goal of the Office of Education in perspective by noting that

> Equal educational opportunity, defined as desegregated education, had become a central—perhaps *the* central—demand of the civil-rights movement by 1950. This strategy in turn led to one of the central Supreme Court decisions of American history, *Brown vs. Board of Education of Topeka*, which declared, in 1954, that "separate but equal" school facilities were inherently *un*equal and ultimately ordered the South to desegregate "with all deliberate speed." At the risk of over-simplifying, it may be stated that the central purpose of the EEOS was to support that strategy and hasten that process.[29]

In the course of the study Coleman and his associates considered five varieties of concepts of equality of educational opportunity.[30] Of the five they considered, however, only two were used in the design of the study. The first was the concept that prevailed before the study was undertaken:

> Stated briefly, before EEOS, "equality of educational opportunity" was measured in terms of school inputs, including racial mixture. By inputs we mean physical facilities of schools and training of teachers; by racial mixture, the Supreme Court's emphasis on integration.[31]

If the study had confirmed what the academic establishment and the Office of Education had believed—that the Negro and other designated minorities were denied equality of educational opportunity because of the poorer quality of "inputs" in their schools—is it likely that the prevailing concept would have been abandoned? Is it not more likely that the concept would have been retained in the above form precisely because it had been proven "operationally useful" in proving that these minorities had, in fact, been denied equal opportunities, and that this denial was the obvious reason for their

consistently poor performance as measured by standardized tests?

What the Coleman survey did find was that no such
significant variance in school inputs as had been imag-
ined to exist was to be found. The survey further found
that such variance as was found had little relation to the
academic achievement of the students. At this point it
may be worth quoting some of Professor Coleman's own
summary at length:

> Even the school-to-school variation in achievement,
> though relatively small, is in itself almost wholly due to
> the *social* environment provided by the school: the educa-
> tional backgrounds and aspirations of other students in
> the school, and the educational backgrounds and attain-
> ments of the teachers in the school. Per-pupil expendi-
> tures, books in the library, and a host of other facilities
> and curricular measures show virtually no relation to
> achievement if the social environment of the school—the
> educational backgrounds of other students and teachers—
> is held constant....Altogether, the sources of inequality
> of educational opportunity appear to lie first in the home
> itself and the cultural influences immediately surrounding
> the home; then they lie in the school's ineffectiveness to
> free achievement from the impact of the home, and in
> the school's cultural homogeneity which perpetuates the
> social influences of the home and its environs.[32]

In terms, then, of the prevailing understanding of
what equality of educational opportunity meant, the
study should have found that the opportunities enjoyed
by the several races were substantially equal, that there
had been no significant denial of opportunities "by reason of race, color, religion, or national origins." Instead,
the authors, intent upon proving the existence of such
deprivation, now changed their conception of equality of
educational opportunity to mean equality of school *out-
puts* as demonstrated by tests of academic achievement.

In other words, so long as all students do not evince equal intelligence by doing equally well in achievement tests we have *prima facie* evidence of the lack of equal educational opportunity. If one person or one group does less well than another, the cause cannot be some genetic or cultural lack but rather a lack of equal opportunity. And there is the implied responsibility of someone else to make up for the lack. Considering that the Civil Rights Act of 1964 "arose largely out of concern for the status of a specific group: the Negro,"[33] perhaps this conclusion is understandable in political terms. In terms of the canons of social science, however, it is a disgrace.

We can readily enough agree with Charles E. Silberman when he says that "the Coleman Report suggests forcibly that the public schools do not—and as now constituted cannot—fulfil what has always been considered to be one of their main purposes and justifications: to ensure equality of opportunity."[34] So long as individuals vary as they do, there can be no such thing as equality of opportunity. An unequal performance is exactly what we would expect from unequal individuals.

Notes

[1] H. M. Kallen, "Behaviorism," *Encyclopaedia of the Social Sciences*, Vol. II, p. 498.

[2] As quoted in Helmut Schoeck, "Individuality v. Equality" in *Essays on Individuality*, ed. by Felix Morley (Philadelphia: University of Pennsylvania Press, 1958), p. 114.

[3] Daniel J. Boorstin, *The Genius of American Politics* (Chicago: The University of Chicago Press, 1953), p. 176.

"One would think, then, that with so much discussion 'about equality,' there would be little vagueness as to what equality itself is about—what one means by 'equality.' Yet this is not at all the case. I think I can best illustrate this point by recounting a couple of my editorial experiences at the journal, *The Public Interest*, with which I am associated.

"It is clear that some Americans are profoundly and sincerely agitated by the existing distribution of income in this country, and these same Americans—they are mostly professors, of course—are constantly insisting that a more equal distribution of income is a matter of considerable urgency. Having myself no strong prior opinion as to the 'proper' shape of an income-distribution curve in such a country as the United States, I have written to several of these professors asking them to compose an article that would describe a proper redistribution of American income. In other words, in the knowledge that they are discontented with our present income distribution, and taking them at their word that when they demand 'more equality' they are not talking about an absolute leveling of all incomes, I invited them to give our readers a picture of what a 'fair' distribution of income would be like.

"I have never been able to get that article, and I have come to the conclusion that I never shall get it. In two cases, I was promised such an analysis, but it was never written. In the other cases, no one was able to find the time to devote to it. Despite all the talk 'about equality,' no one seems willing to commit himself to a precise definition from which statesmen and social critics can take their bearings." Irving Kristol, "About Equality," *Commentary*, Vol. 54, No. 5, (November, 1972), p. 41.

"The issues of schooling, of income, of status have all become matters of social policy because equality has been one of the central values of the American polity. But there has never been a clear-cut meaning to equality, and the earliest form of the idea in the 17th century was quite different from the popular form it assumed in the third decade of the 19th century." Daniel Bell, "On Meritocracy and Equality," *The Public Interest*, No. 29 (Fall, 1972), p. 39.

[4]George Harris, *Inequality and Progress* (Boston: Houghton Mifflin and Co., 1898), pp. 1-2.

[5]Roger J. Williams, *You Are Extraordinary* (New York: Random House, 1967), p. 35.

[6]*Ibid.*, pp. 47-48.

[7]*Ibid.*, pp. 48, 50.

[8]Garrett Hardin, *Nature and Man's Fate* (New York: Rinehart & Company, Inc., 1959), p. 188.

[9]Noting that the American Declaration of Independence was "drafted without conspicuous circumspection because nothing it said could commit any government to any course of action," Nathaniel Weyl points out that "When he wrote the Declaration of Independence, Jefferson may have had George Mason's Virginia Declaration of Rights before him with its preamble 'of a fundamental nature,' asserting that 'all men are by nature equally free and independent.'

"If Jefferson chose the cruder formulation that 'all men are created equal,' thus asserting a proposition he believed false, the reason probably was that he needed phrases able to move men's souls. His task was to wage psychological warfare, an area in which veracity plays a notoriously subordinate role." Nathaniel Weyl, *The Negro in American Civilization* (Washington, D.C.: Public Affairs Press, 1960), p. 36. For a discussion of Jefferson's views on human inequality see Weyl, *op. cit.*, pp. 35-51.

"Jefferson's phrase, presented as a self-evident truth, was false...and so for almost two centuries American thought, with increasing agony and distortion, has been nailed to a cross of revolutionary propaganda, a passing political slogan which its sophisticated author would have been the last to take seriously. Fundamentalist we may no longer be in our religious contemplations. Yet contemporary social theory can yield nothing to mumbling, illiterate, forgotten multitudes in their cringing devotions to antique creeds." Robert Ardrey, *The Social Contract* (New York: Atheneum, 1970), p. 37.

[10]Ardrey, *The Social Contract* pp. 35, 37.

[11]Ludwig von Mises, "On Equality and Inequality," *Modern Age*, Vol. 5, No. 2 (Spring, 1961), p. 140.

[12]Murray N. Rothbard, *Education, Free and Compulsory* (Center for Independent Education, undated), p. 5.

[13]Murray N. Rothbard, *Power and Market* (Menlo Park: The Institute for Humane Studies, Inc., 1970), p.158.

[14]*Idem.*

[15]George Harris, *op. cit.*, p. 21

[16]R. H. Tawney, *Equality* (London: Allen and Unwin, 1931), pp. 129, 143-144.

[17]Blum and Kalven, *The Uneasy Case for Progressive Taxation* (Chicago: The University of Chicago Press, 1953), p. 85.

[18]Leland B. Yeager, "Can a Liberal Be an Egalitarian," in *Toward Liberty* (Menlo Park: The Institute for Humane Studies, Inc., 1971), Vol. 2, p. 425.

[19]Rothbard, *Power and Market*, p. 159.
[20]*Idem.*
"This is one of the reasons why, again and again, collectivists sneer at the institution of the family. It simply does not tie in with the ideal of equality." Schoeck, *loc. cit.* p. 123.

"Recently reemphasized by sociologists, the central role of the family in the handing down of social inequality has been recognized since the time of Plato.

"In the *Republic*, Plato indicated that in the just society it would be necessary to take children away from their parents and have them raised by the state, in order to eliminate the tendency toward inherited social privilege. In the early 19th century, Robert Owen specifically proposed that all children, regardless of the class status of their parents, be educated from childhood in state-supported boarding schools. This suggestion was actually advanced by leaders of the New York Workingmen's party of the 1820s and 1830s. In party documents they argued that since the social environment in families of varying wealth and culture differed greatly, the only chance to insure that the children of the poor had the same chance for success as those of the well-to-do was to send all to public boarding schools. Writing in 1830, these early American radicals, anticipating recent sociological research, held that integrating the children of the rich and the poor in the "common" (integrated) school was not enough. For they argued that the most important part of education goes on outside the classroom:

> For our part, we understand education to mean everything which influences directly or indirectly the child's character. To see his companions smoke segars is a part of his education; to hear oaths is a part of his education; to see and laugh at drunken men in the streets is a part of his education. And if any one thinks that an education like this (which is daily obtained in the streets of our city) will be counteracted and neutralized by half a dozen hours of daily schooling, we are not of his opinion . . . .
>
> Is not the development of social habits, of the dispositions, of the moral feelings, of the most important of the teacher's duties? And what opportunity of fulfilling them, unless the pupil be at all times under his very eye and control?
>
> We conceive, then, that State Schools, to be republican, efficient, and acceptable to all, must receive the children, not six hours a day but altogether; must feed them, clothe them, lodge them, must direct not their studies only, but their occupations and amusements; must care for them until their education is completed, and then abandon them to the world as useful, intelligent, virtuous citizens.
>
> We do not consider the question regarding day schools and boarding schools as a non-essential matter that can be decided either way without ruin to the cause. On its decision depends whether the system of education

which the people call for, shall be a paltry palliative or an efficient cure; whether aristocracy shall be perpetuated or destroyed; whether the poor man's child shall be educated or not; whether the next generation shall obtain their just rights or lose them.

"There are few reformers today who would be prepared to make a suggestion as radical as this one. Perhaps even more than the taking away of children from their parents, the kind of all pervasive moral supervision called for by the New York Workingmen probably seems repugnant even to today's most committed egalitarians. But it is necessary to raise the question of whether these radicals of the 1830s did not see the issue more clearly and reason about it more consistently than many radicals of the 1970s. For if one really wishes a society in which there is not merely formal equality of opportunity but where class background has absolutely no relation to success, one must be willing to pay the necessary price. And that price would appear to include the practical abolition of the family, the suppression of varying cultural and ethnic influences, and a vigorously imposed uniformity in the education of the young. As the Communist experience has shown, the abolition of capitalism, at least in itself, is by no means sufficient." Seymour Martin Lipset, "Social Mobility and Equal Opportunity," *The Public Interest*, No. 29 (Fall, 1972), pp. 106-108.

[21]Rothbard, *Education, Free and Compulsory*, p. 6.

[22]Everett Dean Martin, *The Meaning of a Liberal Education* (Garden City, N.Y.: Garden City Publishing Company, Inc., 1926), pp. 112-113.

[23]Harris, *op. cit.* pp. 43-46.

[24]Colin Greer, *Cobweb Attitudes* (New York: Teachers College Press, Columbia University, 1970), p. 29.

[25]Helmut Schoeck, *Envy* (New York: Harcourt, Brace & World, Inc. 1969), p. 243.

"What is at stake today is the redefinition of equality. A principle which was the weapon for changing a vast social system, the principle of equality of opportunity, is now seen as leading to a new hierarchy, and the current demand is that the 'just precedence' of society, in Locke's phrase, requires the reduction of all inequality, or the creation of *equality of result*—in income, status, and power—for all men in society. This is the central value problem of the post-industrial society." Daniel Bell, "On Meritocracy and Equality," *The Public Interest*, No. 29 (Fall, 1972), p. 40.

[26]James S. Coleman, Ernest A. Campbell, Carol J. Hobson, James McPartland, Alexander N. Mood, Frederic D. Wainfield, Robert L. York, *Equality of Educational Opportunity*, 2 volumes (Washington, D.C.: U.S. Government Printing Office, 1966) Superintendent of Documents Catalog No. FS 5.238: 38001.

[27]Frederick Mosteller and Daniel P. Moynihan, editors, *On Equality of Educational Opportunity* (New York: Vintage Books, a Division of Random House, 1972).

[28]Mosteller and Moynihan, "A Pathbreaking Report," *Ibid.,* p. 5.

"The Office of Education, which sponsored the research, and Coleman himself had expected to find gross inequality of educational resources between black and white schools and to use these findings as an argument for large scale federal spending to redress the balance." Daniel Bell, "On Meritocracy and Equality," *The Public Interest*, No. 29, (Fall, 1972), p. 44.

[29]*Ibid.*, pp. 29-30.

[30]James S. Coleman, "The Evaluation of *Equality of Educational Opportunity*, in Mosteller and Moynihan, *op. cit.*, p. 147. See also Coleman, "The Concept of Equality of Educational Opportunity," *Harvard Educational Review*, 38, Winter 1968, pp. 7-22; Edmund W. Gordon, "Toward Defining Equality of Educational Opportunity," and Henry S. Dyer, "The Measurement of Educational Opportunity," in Mosteller and Moynihan, *op. cit.*, pp. 423-436, 513-527.

[31]Mosteller and Moynihan, "A Pathbreaking Report," *op. cit.*, p. 6.

[32]As quoted in Mosteller and Moynihan, "A Pathbreaking Report," *op. cit.*, p. 20.

[33]*Ibid.*, p. 30.

[34]Charles E. Silberman, "A Devastating Report on U.S. Education," *Fortune*, August 1967, p. 181, quoted in Mosteller and Moynihan, "A Pathbreaking Report," *op. cit.*, p. 30.

Attorney Gerrit H. Wormhoudt examines the crucial Supreme Court cases that have expanded or delimited compulsion in education. He discovers a heartening— but shaky—trend toward diversity, freedom, and the sovereignty of parents. But, he notes, the court is a long way from abandoning compulsion altogether or curbing the arrogance of the educational establishment.

Supreme Court Decisions

Gerrit H. Wormhoudt

I intend to explore the limits, under the United States Constitution, upon the modes of governmental force that may be brought to bear against the rights of people to choose for themselves the manner and content of the education their children will receive.

In legal parlance, compulsory schooling is usually equated with state truancy laws. Truancy statutes typically impose criminal penalties upon parents who do not cause their children to receive, during specified ages, the kind and quantity of education required by state laws.

These statutes employ the direct, mailed-fist approach to accomplishing minimum governmental schooling objectives. Parents are given no choice, short of fine or imprisonment, in satisfying the seemingly limited standards set forth in the truancy statutes of the state where they and their children may reside, unless refusal to comply can be constitutionally justified.

It is best to say at the outset, however, that the actual reach of government-compelled schooling obviously far exceeds the domain strictly encompassed by state truancy laws. Those laws cannot be fully appreciated if they are viewed in isolation from the other coercive powers of government that impinge upon freedom of education.

Suppose some state, say New York, should establish its own publishing enterprise administered by its State Department of Public Information, so that all citizens could have without cost, except, of course, for taxes paid, government-published counterparts of the *New York Times, Saturday Review, Fortune* Magazine, and, eventually, the intended equivalents of all periodicals, books, and other literature now privately published, other than sectarian works. There would be no direct tax upon private publishers, but they would have to be self-supporting while their government competition would be sustained by some general tax assessment constituting an indistinguishable but ever-increasing portion of the state budget. Next, the state offers to subsidize struggling private publishers who agree, in exchange for the receipt of public funds, to conform to New York's minimum standards of objective, truthful, and desirable publishing. Further, suppose that New York eventually requires every citizen, under penalty of fine or imprisonment, to devote so much time each week, regardless of his reading speed, to the study of prescribed information published by accredited publishing houses employing only certified writers, all in accordance with the accreditation and certification standards established and administered by the New York State Department of Public Information. All of this would rest on New York's legitimate interest in a well informed and self-sustaining electorate, and on every citizen's right to equality of information.

With these rights fully secured, another set of rights becomes increasingly important. As New York's publishing business has expanded at a geometrical rate, and the tax levies necessary for its sustenance have grown apace and have become second only to those required for public school support, the tens of thousands of certified employees of the Department of Public Information have become increasingly restless. They have not only obtained their constitutional right to organize and engage in professional negotiations concerning wages, hours, and other terms and conditions of employment, but they are threatening to strike unless their demands for permanent tenure and for full control of accreditation and certification standards are met. Since their union has affiliated with the NEA and AFT to form the Professional Mind Workers of America, there is the chance that all sources of information in New York may at least temporarily shut down. The overwhelming majority of the employees of public schools, of government-supported private schools, and of government-supported private publishers, have been certified and organized, and they are honor-bound to strike in sympathy with the demands of their certified brethren employed by the Department of Public Information. If the strike does come to pass, it is predicted that the administration of criminal justice in New York may be pushed to the point of collapse as it attempts to prosecute all those parents who will be in violation of the school truancy act and all of its residents who fail to fulfil their minimum obligations under the compulsory reading act.

If this hypothetical exercise seems either frightening or specious, how does it differ from the real, live American school scene at this moment, except as to the merger of the hypothetical with presently existing professional associations? Are not the actual effects of government's present role as schoolmaster accurately suggested by this imaginary portrayal of government as publisher?

Legal compulsion in schooling occurs whenever government coerces, directly or indirectly, individual choice as to who must go to school, what must be taught, who will be permitted to teach, and which school gets how much money. Truancy statutes are the direct and overt means employed by government to control these choices, but they are by no means the most effective weapon in the government arsenal. The use of tax powers to absorb privately generated funds for the primary use of government schools, the granting of public subsidies to non-governmental schools, conditioned upon their meeting government standards; the threat of denial of tax exemptions to schools that do not conform to government standards—these are all established methods of government coercion in schooling that both complement compulsory attendance statutes and would probably lead to the same near-monopoly of schooling by government existing today, even if there were no truancy statutes.

The Supreme Court, in *Pierce v. Society of Sisters*,[1] held that no truancy law could constitutionally compel parents to send their children to public schools for the satisfaction of a state's minimum schooling requirements. But the *Pierce* decision was handed down nearly fifty years ago, at a time when a great many Americans could afford to pay the price of both a public and private education for their children, if they did not choose to send their children to government schools. With the notable but diminishing exception of our Roman Catholics, today relatively few parents can afford to shoulder the costs of private tuition after they have been compelled to pay through taxation the costs of maintaining government schools. The constitutionally-guaranteed alternative of non-governmental schooling, set forth in the *Pierce* case, has been foreclosed to most parents by another form of government compulsion which has indirectly, but very effectively, vitiated this right by making its exercise a practical impossibility.

As independent schools struggle to retain a clientele who are required to pay a double price if they send their children to non-governmental schools, these schools become increasingly vulnerable to the lure of government aid. Drowning men and independent schools are free to reject any offers of rescue, but the will to survive usually prevails. The price of survival invariably amounts to government control of the recipient school's activities. In his opinion for the court invalidating on First Amendment grounds the efforts of Rhode Island and Pennsylvania to use tax funds to foot some of the costs of secular education in parochial schools, Chief Justice Burger wrote the message plainly:

> The history of government grants of a continuing cash subsidy indicates that such programs have almost always been accompanied by varying measures of control and surveillance.[2]

Although we supposedly enjoy the blessings attendant upon an age of legal realism, whatever restraints there are today upon the power of taxation are largely matters of form and not of practical consequence. If a state were foolish enough to impose a tax upon the right of a parent to send his child to a non-governmental school, the tax would doubtless be unlawful, since, in the words of Justice Douglas:

> A state may not impose a charge for the enjoyment of a right granted by the Federal Constitution.[3]

However, in the same, opinion, the author distinguished the tax in question, a license tax imposed upon door-to-door solicitors, applied to Jehovah's Witnesses, from a uniform tax on property or income not specifically aimed at the exercise of a constitutional right:

> It is one thing to impose a tax on the income or property of a preacher. It is quite another thing to exact a tax from him for the privilege of delivering a sermon.[4]

Hence, a uniform tax levied for support of public schools displays on its surface no constitutional infirmity, even though the consequence of such a tax may be the confiscation of the financial ability (of all persons who do not command above-average resources) to exercise the constitutional right to patronize private schools.

Before concluding, however, that the Constitution provides no protection whatsoever against confiscatory, but non-discriminatory, taxation of the economic resources necessary to provide any substance to the constitutional right to choose non-governmental schooling, I should mention that there is at least some basis for hoping to the contrary. While it is ever risky to separate what any court has said from the context of the facts that occasioned the remarks, attempts to do just this are irresistible, especially when the words are what one wants to hear. What has been said before by a court, regardless of context, at least tends to require serious thought, if it is to be explained away on subsequent occasions when it is invoked as applicable. Writing for the court in a case decided in 1972, holding that under the original Civil Rights Act personal rights to liberty are inseparable from personal rights in property, Mr. Justice Stewart said:

> In fact, a fundamental interdependence exists between the personal right to liberty and the personal right in property. Neither could have meaning without the other.[5]

Now, compare Justice Stewart's statement with the language used by Justice Brennan in his concurring opinion in a First Amendment case that held unconstitutional a Pennsylvania statute requiring Bible reading in public schools:

> Attendance at the public schools has never been compulsory; parents remain morally and constitutionally free to choose the academic environment in which they wish their children to be educated. The relationship of the Establishment Clause of the First Amendment to the public school system is preeminently that of reserving such a choice to the individual parent, rather than vesting it in the majority of voters of each state or school district. The choice which is thus preserved is between a public secular education with its uniquely democratic values, and some form of private or sectarian education, which offers values of its own. In my judgment the First Amendment forbids the state to inhibit that freedom of choice by diminishing the attractiveness of either alternative—either by restricting the liberty of the private schools to inculcate whatever values they wish, or by jeopardizing the freedom of the public schools from private or sectarian pressures. The choice between these very different forms of education is one—very much like the choice of whether or not to worship—which our Constitution leaves to the individual parent. It is no proper function of the state or local gov-

ernment to influence or restrict that election. The lesson
of history—drawn more from the experiences of other
countries than from our own—is that a system of free
public education forfeits its unique contribution to the
growth of democratic citizenship when that choice ceases
to be freely available to each parent.[6]

Faced with the above language, would not Justices
Stewart and Brennan, at least, be required to give serious consideration to the plight of a parent whose limited
income prevents him from electing to send his child to a
parochial school after he has paid through taxes all or
part of the cost of sending his child to a public school?
Has not the government in such circumstances inhibited,
and in fact eliminated, the exercise of a choice the Constitution supposedly guarantees?

And how would Justice Douglas, confronted with such
a case, explain away his position set forth as follows in
Murdock v. Pennsylvania:

> This tax is not a charge for the enjoyment of a privilege
> or benefit bestowed by the state. The privilege in question
> exists apart from state authority. It is guaranteed the peo-
> ple by the Federal Constitution.[7]

Perhaps the justice might answer by saying that a general tax to support the public schools is a charge for a
privilege bestowed by the government. But such an answer invites this obvious question in rejoinder: "Why
should the state be empowered to destroy the constitutionally guaranteed right to choose parochial schooling
under the guise of conferring a privilege or benefit
upon anyone or everyone?" Justice Douglas joined in
Justice Black's concurring opinion in *Lemon v. Kurtzman* (Note 2), which emphasized that the financing of
secular activities in a parochial school amounts to a subsidy of its sectarian programs by releasing additional

funds for them, and that to ignore these consequences "...makes a grave constitutional decision turn merely on cost accounting and bookkeeping entries."[8] This logic is surely sound, and it serves to eliminate any realistic distinction between a direct tax upon the right to pursue non-governmental schooling and a tax uniformly levied for support of government schools. It is all the same to the individual taxpayer's pocketbook whether the amount he must pay for public school support is denominated a charge for a government-bestowed benefit, or a tax upon his right to send his children to schools operating independently of government. In either case, he has no choice as to how his resources available for education will be spent, notwithstanding his supposed constitutional right to choose private schools.

In his *Murdock* opinion Justice Douglas also said:

> Freedom of speech, freedom of the press, freedom of religion are available to all, not merely to those who can pay their own way."[9]

If this is true, then it must be a further truth, and surely a more profound truth, that those who might afford to pay their own way in exercising a constitutional right may not be deprived by the state of their financial ability to do so, without a compelling reason to the contrary. No contrary reason can possibly be supported. Authorizing a parent who opts for private schooling to retain that part of his school tax bill, only to the extent that it would cost the public schools to educate his children, would not deprive the public treasury of any funds, since the money retained by the taxpayer would merely equal the savings to the public. Nor could such retention of funds by a taxpayer properly be called a tax exemption, to be granted or withheld as a matter of grace. It would simply amount to the unfettering of a constitutionally-guaranteed choice, permitting a taxpayer to spend his resources at a public or private school, as he sees fit, but only so long as he has children of school age. If this reasoning has ever been urged upon the court, its opinions do not so reflect.

During 1973, the Supreme Court in *Sloan v. Lemon,*[10] *Levitt v. Committee for Public Education,*[11] and *Nyquist v. Committee for Public Education,*[12] considered a series of state enactments from New York and from Pennsylvania which were designed to alleviate in part the dollar pressures imposed by government upon parents to forsake private education for their children. In the *Levitt* case, the court held that the First Amendment precludes reimbursement by a state to private schools for the cost of testing and record keeping requirements mandated by the state. For the same reason, in the *Sloan* and *Nyquist* cases, the court invalidated partial private school tuition reimbursements to parents, limited state tax relief to taxpaying parents whose children attend private school, and fractional state payments to private schools for their costs of maintenance and repair of facilities. All of these enactments were viewed as violations of the First Amendment proscription against an establishment of religion. Not a single justice, including the three dissenters, Burger, White and Rehnquist, discussed the relation between this legislation and the constitutionally protected right of parents to select nongovernmental schools for their children. The justices only disagreed as to whether aid to parents amounted to prohibited religion subsidies and as to whether the New York tax relief program amounted to tax credits, deductions, or exemptions, and if exemptions, whether the court's holding was consistent with its previous approval in *Walz v. Tax*

Commission[13] of exemption from state real estate taxes for church property. Nor was mention made of the court's earlier 1973 decision in *San Antonio School District v. Rodriguez*,[14] which held that government provision of education is consistent with, but is not required by, the federal constitution. Seemingly, the court has implicitly said that, while government has no constitutional duty to educate, it has unlimited power to do so, and if such power is used to appropriate the dollars available for effective exercise of the fundamental right of parents to avoid governmentally dispensed education for their children, the First Amendment precludes any disgorgement of those funds. While the court has never said this explicitly, it must be admited that its recent decisions provide slim hope that the court will soon, if ever, recognize that, in Justice Stewart's language, the constitutional right to choose private education and the right to apply one's education dollars, so as to make the first right meaningful, are mutually interdependent.

The devices available to government for enforcing school attendance are easily laid bare, but intelligibly defining the content of what may be compelled by government in the name of "education" is altogether another matter. The First Amendment school cases decided by the Supreme Court suggest that the problem may be insoluble. Because the First Amendment to the Constitution applies to all levels of government, neither federal, state, nor local officials may establish religion or prohibit the free exercise thereof; and, neither may they abridge freedom of speech or of the press. In a continuing stream of decisions, the Supreme Court is being called upon to decide whether some particular practice or prohibition enforced in the public schools, or some attempt to give public funds to parochial schools, runs contrary

to First Amendment mandates. In so doing, the court
has made basic assumptions as to "educational" processes
which are, to put it mildly, open to question. Those assumptions are also inconsistent with what the court has
held on other occasions.

Whenever the Supreme Court has been faced with a
claim that some practice in the public schools violates either the establishment clause or the free exercise clause
of the First Amendment, or that public funding of parochial schools does so, it has premised its decision on the
explicit ground that there is a knowable line of demarca-
tion between secular education and sectarian education,
however difficult it may be to locate the boundary. The
First Amendment is said to confine government-supported schools to the teaching of secular subjects, and as a
corollary, it is construed to sanction government funding
of sectarian-controlled schools to the extent of their dispensation of secular education, provided that, in any
given case of public aid, government can avoid excessive
entanglement with the religious activities of sectarian
schools. The herculean nature of the task imposed by
these guidelines becomes apparent from even a superficial examination of the problems that have been presented to the court for solution.

In *Board of Education v. Allen*, the court applied the
secular-sectarian test in determining the validity of a
New York statute which entailed the loan of publicly-
purchased textbooks to all school children in grades 7
through 12, including those in attendance at parochial
schools. In practice, all such books were approved by
public school authorities, and supposedly only secular
texts were approved, although parochial school officials
suggested texts for approval. None of the texts in issue
was reviewed in the majority opinion. Accordingly, the

court avoided passing judgment upon the actual con-
tents of any text, and so it was able to conclude, as an
abstract proposition, that public funding of texts for parochial schools does not violate the First Amendment:

> However, the language of § 701 does not authorize the
> loan of religious books, and the state claims no right to
> distribute religious literature. Although the books loaned
> are those required by the parochial school for use in spe-
> cific courses, each book loaned must be approved by the
> public school authorities; only secular books may receive
> approval. The law was construed by the Court of Appeals
> of New York as "merely making available secular text-
> books at the the request of the individual student," supra,
> and the record contains no suggestion that religious books
> have been loaned. Absent evidence, we cannot assume
> that school authorities, who constantly face the same
> problem in selecting textbooks for use in the public
> schools, are unable to distinguish between secular and re-
> ligious books or that they will not honestly discharge their
> duties under the law. In judging the validity of the statute
> on this record we must proceed on the assumption that
> books loaned to students are books that are not unsuitable
> for use in the public schools because of religious content.[15]

Justice Douglas and Justice Black dissented. Justice
Douglas refused to wear the blinders provided by abstract conceptions of the secular and the sectarian. He
cited numerous illustrations of texts treating with a religious flavor supposedly secular subjects such as biology,
economics, government, and history. Justice Douglas
said out loud what other members of the court also
surely know to be true. Every textbook on almost any
subject will tend to reflect value judgments on the part
of the writer and the teacher or other authority who
selects it for use:

> Even where the treatment given to a particular topic in a
> school textbook is not blatantly sectarian, it will necessarily

have certain shadings that will lead a parochial school to prefer one text over another.[16]

But Justice Douglas' argument proves too much. If sectarian school officials tend to let their dogmas influence the selection of texts, what may be said of public school officials? Some of the standards set by New York for guiding the judgment of public officials in the selection of suitable texts are mentioned in Justice Douglas' dissent. They deserve full quotation:

> The material is to "promote the objectives of the educational program," "treat the subject competently and accurately," "be in good taste," "have a wholesome tone that is consonant with right conduct and civic values," "be in harmony with American democratic ideals and moral values," "be free of any reflection on the dignity and status of any group, race, or religion, whether expressed or implied, by statement or omission," and "be free of objectionable features of over-dramatization, violence, or crime." *Guiding Principles for Schools in the Selection and Use of "Non-Listed" Instructional Materials* (1952).[17]

The challenged New York law leaves to the Board of Regents, local boards of education, trustees, and other school authorities the supervision of the textbook program. The Board of Regents (together with the commissioner of education) has powers of censorship over all textbooks that contain statements seditious in character, or evince disloyalty to the United States or are favorable to any nation with which we are at war. (New York Education Law § 704.) Those powers can cut a wide swath in many areas of education that involve the ideological element.[18]

When the court has been faced with questions as to the constitutionality of specific state action dealing with curriculum content, its burden of judgment is painfully

clear. Even an Arkansas statute prohibiting the teaching
of evolution presented obvious difficulties for a court
that does not wish to find itself sitting as a board of review for all public school materials. In *Epperson v. Arkansas*, the majority of the court struck down the law as
offensive to the First Amendment, but Justice Black,
while concurring, expressed his doubts as to the position
the court was assuming:

> However wise this court may be or may become hereafter,
> it is doubtful that, sitting in Washington, it can successful-
> ly supervise and censor the curriculum of every public
> school in every hamlet and city in the United States. I
> doubt that our wisdom is so nearly infallible.[19]

The secular-sectarian dichotomy used by the court has
also been applied to teacher qualifications. In *Lemon v.
Kurtzman*, the chief justice attempted to distinguish the
constitutionally permissible funding of textbooks for parochial schools from impermissible public support of sectarian teachers:

> In *Allen* the court refused to make assumptions, on a
> meager record, about the religious content of the text-
> books that the state would be asked to provide. We can-
> not, however, refuse here to recognize that teachers have
> a substantially different ideological character from books.
> In terms of potential for involving some aspect of faith or
> morals in secular subjects, a textbook's content is ascer-
> tainable, but a teacher's handling of a subject is not. We
> cannot ignore the danger that a teacher under religious
> control and discipline poses to the separation of the reli-
> gious from the purely secular aspects of precollege educa-
> tion. The conflict of functions inheres in the situation.[20]

Again the question comes up: if sectarian teachers
may pose a threat to constitutional freedoms, what of
their public school counterparts? The court has said that
the public schools may not make a religion of secular-

ism.[21] But can a teacher's qualifications to teach secular subjects in a manner that does not make secularism a religion be determined by judges or any other public official?

The decisions of the court mentioned heretofore may be viewed as an attempt to define the secular education that is constitutionally permissible in public schools, by eliminating from it any sectarian influences on a case-by-case basis. In this fashion, the court may indefinitely evade examination of the positive issues inherent in the very nature of schooling.

Dispassionate teachers and dispassionate text writers are as rare as dispassionate judges. In everything that passes for schooling, the views of some particular sect will hold sway, whether that sect be characterized as religious, secular, political, philosophical, or whatever. The range of possibilities is as unlimited as the scope of knowledge, belief, emotion and individual preferences and prejudices. Is it anything other than simple honesty to admit that this is so? The changing character of the public schools provides incontestable proof. The rural and urban neighborhood public schools of not long ago were descendants of denominational schools, most often Protestant in origin. As such, they long continued to ignore any distinction between the secular and the sectarian, until occasionally forced to do otherwise. Those earlier schools also reflected in large measure the values of relatively close-knit communities which also fully sustained them financially. Those who funded the localized schools of yesterday, rightly or wrongly, controlled the content of curriculum, the selection of faculty, and the values that were disseminated.

Both state and federal officials these days assume an ever-growing role in shaping the character of today's schools. Uniform standards of curriculum and faculty are promulgated from ever higher levels in ever increasing detail. School expenditures represent the single largest item in total governmental budgeting for domestic measures. Needless to say, the governmental power and resources devoted to education are not dispensed in a vacuum. Hundreds of thousands of educationists are dependent upon public finance for their income. Whoever controls the public school structure is in a position to manage the shaping of the minds of all but a handful of our children. These controllers and their interests and values need to be identified if there is to be any realistic assessment of the constitutional dimensions of freedom of choice in American schools.

The fact is that members of the teaching profession are the only certain beneficiaries of public expenditures for schooling. The power of government can be used to create and perpetuate an educationist establishment with monopolistic privileges, just as it can be used to favor business by protective tariffs and subsidies. Likewise, government-imposed standards for accreditation of schools and certification of teachers can be promulgated in the name of the public interest in better schools and teachers, as tariffs are often said to be imposed in order to make the nation safe from its enemies. But in each such case, we do well to seek the identity of those who will measurably benefit from the governmental undertaking in question.

Massive teachers' unions are no different from other groups bonded by a common economic interest. However, they do enjoy prerogatives of a special nature which stem from the paramount interest of all in matters affecting children. Because of common concern that some parents might fail to provide their children with what everyone supposedly knows and recognizes as at least a minimum education, public schools were initiated for the benefit of the children of such neglectful parents. Later, this sentiment gave rise to truancy statutes. These early, limited ventures by government into schooling were usually consistent with the common-law role of the state as *parens patriae*. Under this doctrine, parents were charged with both the right and obligation to sustain and educate their children, and only when that right had been forfeited in a specific instance of neglect, could government intervene in the parent-child relationship.

> Every statute which is designed to give protection, care, and training to children, as a needed substitute for parental authority and performance of parental duty, is but a recognition of the duty of the state, as the legitimate guardian and protector of children where other guardianship fails.[22]

Building upon such seemingly innocuous premises to justify limited government compulsion of minimum schooling requirements for those children whose parents either could not or would not privately assume them, the proponents of public education have used governmental powers to create an educationist establishment that is approaching monopoly proportions. Chief Justice Burger's aside in *Lemon v. Kurtzman* is appropriate here, and it demonstrates a remarkable ability for understatement:

> We have already noted that modern governmental programs have self-perpetuating and self-expanding propensities.[23]

Schooling today has almost wholly ceased to be a matter of parental control; instead, it is developing into an exclusive domain for professionals who claim for themselves alone the necessary expertise for formulating standards for teachers and schools, and who are sufficient in number and in political influence to see that government enforces the standards they develop. If political action fails, they can assert their coming right to strike against parents and children, who are compelled by truancy laws and taxation to patronize the very schools that teachers, it is claimed, must have the right to boycott if their demands are not met. Ironically, it is still open to question whether the neglected child receives any more or better schooling today than he did before the creation of the present vast structure that government originated for this limited purpose.

The point to this seeming digression from the Supreme Court's attempt to define secular and sectarian education is simply this: formal schooling of children today is almost entirely a product fashioned by an elite group that has a tremendous stake in ever larger public school budgets, but very little accountability to anyone for what happens in the name of public schooling. Their views of history, economics, government, and the nature of man and society dominate the curriculum and the manner of its dispensation, both in public schools and in those private schools that comply with government standards in order to receive public aid. Generalizations as to the common values of any group are suspect, but at least certain obvious questions are in order as to teachers who depend upon government compulsion for their livelihood. Will they not by virtue of their own commissions be partial to versions of history that favor governmental intervention as the necessary and proper solution to man's recurring problems? Will the nineteenth century be portrayed as a period when purported excesses of economic freedom led to clearly undesirable social conditions, or will those results be attributed to the already growing tendency of government to interfere with the free market by using its powers to favor first one special interest and then another? Will the early twentieth century be seen as an age of reform when government tamed economic monopolies, or as a period when wavering economic concentrations obtained governmental suppression of competition under the guise of industry regulations needed for businesses affected with a public interest? Will the crash of 1929 be told as a story of private greed and irresponsible speculation without mention of the use of governmental monetary policy to encourage those very propensities? Will the ensuing depression years be recounted as the longest period of economic suffering in American history, terminated only by a world war, or as a time when massive government intervention provided balance to the American economy?

Even more important questions need to be asked about these beneficiaries of government compulsion. How will they tend to depict the nature of those beings who are subject to their teaching? Will they be seen as responsible, moral agents, endowed with that capacity for conscious choice that gives rise to a system of individually oriented ethical and legal rights and obligations, or will man be viewed as a mobile intersection of biological and environmental happenings, a mere plastic object to be shaped and directed as is any other segment of a material universe? Are the "education" courses and the teaching methods posited by legally established teacher certification requirements based upon the view that men are endowed with neither dignity nor freedom, unless, perchance, they are members of the educationist establishment? Professional educationists as distant in time as

Plato and his present heirs, Galbraith and Skinner, have fashioned utopias in which philosopher kings wisely and infallibly use the powers of government to provide happiness and virtue for the lesser creatures who inhabit their realms. The works of John Dewey, the father of modern education, are consistently directed to the displacement of supernatural agencies in the affairs of man in favor of Dewey's own *summum bonum*, scientific methodology, or the method of intelligence, to use his terminology:

> But generalized agnosticism is only a half-way elimination of the supernatural. Its meaning departs when the intellectual outlook is directed wholly to the natural world. When it is so directed, there are plenty of particular matters regarding which we must say we do not know; we only inquire and form hypotheses which future inquiry will confirm or reject. But such doubts are an incident of faith in the method of intelligence. They are signs of faith, not of a pale and impotent skepticism. We doubt in order that we may find out, not because some inaccessible supernatural lurks behind whatever we can know.[24]

> Here are all the elements for a religious faith that shall not be confined to sect, class, or race. Such a faith has always been implicitly the common faith of mankind. It remains to make it explicit and militant.[25]

Whether the views of Galbraith, Skinner, Dewey, or anyone else have become an unofficial dogma for modern educationists, a dogma that is uniformly dispensed by them through institutions that are governmentally supported, is not the critical point to be made here. Nor do I suggest that the courts or any other body should attempt to investigate this hypothesis. The important thing is to recognize that all teaching and all teachers are laden with values and beliefs that touch upon every aspect of human destiny:

> We should not let ourselves be deceived by the belief that
> public schools are neutral about religion. Neutral they are
> not. By the necessity of the nature which pulsates and
> breathes in pupils, teachers, and parents as human
> beings, every school fosters some form of devotion. The
> religion that inspires a public school, despite the pose of
> neutrality, will be one of the traditional faiths, or a cru-
> sading zeal for social reform, or some other holy cause.[26]

This so obvious fact cannot be indefinitely ignored by
resort to legal classifications such as the secular and the
sectarian to obscure what actually takes place in any
schooling institution.

In another series of cases, which deal with exemptions
from military service based upon religious beliefs, the
Supreme Court has officially recognized that matters of
faith cannot be classified in terms of sectarian or secular
labels. Notwithstanding the explicit congressional denial
of exemption from military conscription to conscientious
objectors whose views are based only upon secular beliefs, the court has construed the exemption provision to
include those whose beliefs are deeply and profoundly
held, regardless of their secular origin:

> In applying § 6(j)'s exclusion of those whose views are
> "essentially political, sociological, or philosophical" or of
> those who have a "merely personal moral code," it should
> be remembered that these exclusions are definitional and
> do not therefore restrict the category of persons who are
> conscientious objectors by "religious training and belief."
> Once the Selective Service System has taken the first step
> and determined under the standards set out here and in
> Seeger that the registrant is a "religious" conscientious ob-
> jector, it follows that his views cannot be "essentially polit-
> ical, sociological, or philosophical."[27]

If the Supreme Court's school decisions are tested by results, rather than by reasons given, it is arguable that the

court itself has not been bound by the labels it has purported to apply. The *Pierce* decision involved more than the right of parents to choose religious schools for their children. Both a Catholic school and a non-denominational military school were parties to the case, and the court's classic statements therein must be read as a guarantee of the right to non-governmental schooling, whether or not it is sponsored by a church. The stated premise of the court speaks to the liberty of individuals and of rights independent of religious affiliation:

> Under the doctrine of *Meyer v. Nebraska*, 262 U.S. 390, 67 L.Ed. 1042, 29 A.L.R. 1446, 43 Sup. Ct. Rep. 625, we think it entirely plain that the Act of 1922 unreasonably interferes with the liberty of parents and guardians to direct the upbringing and education of children under their control. As often heretofore pointed out, rights guaranteed by the Constitution may not be abridged by legislation which has no reasonable relation to some purpose within the competency of the state. The fundamental theory of liberty upon which all governments in this Union repose excludes any general power of the state to standardize its children by forcing them to accept instruction from public teachers only. The child is not the mere creature of the state; those who nurture him and direct his destiny have the right, coupled with the high duty, to recognize and prepare him for additional obligations.[28]

Earlier, in *Meyer v. Nebraska,* the court had invalidated a state statute that prohibited the teaching of modern foreign languages to children below certain ages. The act had been inspired by anti-German sentiment following World War I. The court was not concerned with any problems of religious freedom. Its holding was based upon the ground that the individual has the fundamental right under the Constitution to direct the education of his children:

That the state may do much, go very far, indeed, in order to improve the quality of its citizens, physically, mentally, and morally, is clear; but the individual has certain fundamental rights which must be respected....For the welfare of his Ideal Commonwealth, Plato suggested a law which should provide: "That the wives of our guardians are to be common, and their children are to be common, and no parent is to know his own child nor any child his parent....The proper officers will take the offspring of the good parents to the pen or fold, and there they will deposit them with certain nurses who dwell in a separate quarter; but the offspring of the inferior, or of the better when they chance to be deformed, will be put away in some mysterious, unknown place, as they should be." In order to submerge the individual and develop ideal citizens, Sparta assembled the males at seven into barracks and intrusted their subsequent education and training to official guardians. Although such measures have been deliberately approved by men of great genius, their ideas touching the relation between individual and state were wholly different from those upon which our institutions rest; and it hardly will be affirmed that any legislature could impose such restrictions upon the people of a state without doing violence to both letter and spirit of the Constitution.[29]

In keeping with the *Meyer* and *Pierce* cases is the decision of the court in *Farrington v. Tokushige.* There the territorial legislature of Hawaii had acted to dominate private schools being conducted by orientals in their own tongues. In addition to requiring such schools to obtain licenses from the public school department, the enactment made teaching in such schools conditional upon a pledge to abide by all of the terms of the act and regulations of the department and to "so direct the minds and studies of pupils in such schools as will tend to make them good and loyal American citizens."[30]

The public school officials were also required to select

suitable textbooks for such schools. The Supreme Court said:

> The foregoing statement is enough to show that the School Act and the measures adopted thereunder go far beyond mere regulation of privately supported schools where children obtain instruction deemed valuable by their parents and which is not obviously in conflict with any public interest. They give affirmative direction concerning the intimate and essential details of such schools, intrust their control to public officers, and deny both owners and patrons reasonable choice and discretion in respect of teachers, curriculum and textbooks. Enforcement of the act probably would destroy most, if not all, of them; and, certainly, it would deprive parents of fair opportunity to procure for their children instruction which they think important and we cannot say is harmful. The Japanese parent has the right to direct the education of his own child without unreasonable restrictions; the Constitution protects him as well as those who speak another tongue.[31]

The latest Supreme Court decision dealing with compulsory education is *Wisconsin v. Yoder*. Quite consciously striving to rest its decision on the narrowest possible grounds, the court affirmed the holding of the Supreme Court of Wisconsin that Amish parents would be exempted from the literal terms of Wisconsin's compulsory attendance laws after their children had passed the eighth grade. Because the court placed considerable emphasis upon the peculiarities of Amish doctrine, basing its decision solely upon the free exercise clause of the First Amendment, the *Yoder* case may well be, in the words of Judge Learned Hand, one of those "cases where the occasion is at once the justification for, and the limit of, what is decided."[32] While Chief Justice Burger concluded that Wisconsin's interest in compulsory education was not sufficient to override the religious interests of the Amish, he added these comments:

> A way of life, however virtuous and admirable, may not be interposed as a barrier to reasonable state regulation of education if it is based on purely secular considerations; to have the protection of the Religion Clauses, the claims must be rooted in religious belief. Although a determination of what is a "religious" belief or practice entitled to constitutional protection may present a most delicate question, the very concept of ordered liberty precludes allowing every person to make his own standards on matters of conduct in which society as a whole has important interests. Thus, if the Amish asserted their claims because of their subjective evaluation and rejection of the contemporary secular values accepted by the majority, much as Thoreau rejected the social values of his time and isolated himself at Walden Pond, their claim would not rest on a religious basis. Thoreau's choice was philosophical and personal rather than religious, and such belief does not rise to the demands of the Religion Clause.[33]

The use here by the chief justice of such analytical shibboleths as secular and religious, and his apparent submergence of individual choice in schooling under the weight of the government's interest in compulsory schooling, are in keeping with the sentiments expressed by Justice White in a concurring opinion, in which he was joined by Justices Stewart and Brennan:

> As recently as last term, the court re-emphasized the legitimacy of the state's concern for enforcing minimum educational standards, *Lemon v. Kurtzman,* 403 U.S. 602, 613 (1971). *Pierce v. Society of Sisters,* 268 U.S. 510 (1925), lends no support to the contention that parents may replace state educational requirements with their own idiosyncratic views of what knowledge a child needs to be a productive and happy member of society; in *Pierce,* both the parochial and military schools were in compliance with all the educational standards which the state had set, and the court held simply that while a state

may posit such standards, it may not pre-empt the educational process by requiring children to attend public schools.[34]

With due deference to Justice White, the *Pierce* decision simply did not rule upon the right of the government to set the educational standards for private schools. Justice McReynolds plainly stated in *Pierce* that those requirements were not an issue in the case, while his subsequent opinion in the *Farrington* case plainly holds that fundamental parental rights may not be overridden by governmental standards. Furthermore, there was no evidence before the court in the *Yoder* case, or in any other case of record, which could support the inference of Justice White that state standards may establish "the knowledge a child needs to be a productive and happy member of society."

Justice Douglas, in partial dissent, evidenced his paramount concern for the student's choice rather than that of the parents. However, he was quick to point out that the majority justification of its holding on the basis of traditional Amish religious belief was squarely inconsistent with the decisions of the court in the draft exemption cases.

The *Yoder* case can be read as a forecast of doom for those who believe that the combination of compulsion and schooling are the grave-markers of freedom in any society, even though, thereafter, its members may be taught that they are free by those who forcibly control the development of their beliefs. And yet the basic tenet expressed in the *Pierce* decision was explicitly approved by the court. The Chief Justice also said:

> The history and culture of western civilization reflect a strong tradition of parental concern for the nurture and upbringing of their children. This primary role of the

parents in the upbringing of their children is now established beyond debate as an enduring American tradition....However read, the court's holding in *Pierce* stands as a charter of the rights of parents to direct the religious upbringing of their children. And, when the interests of parenthood are combined with a free exercise claim of the nature revealed by this record, more than merely a "reasonable relation to some purpose within the competency of the state" is required to sustain the validity of the state's requirement under the First Amendment. To be sure, the power of the parent, even when linked to a free exercise claim, may be subject to limitation under *Pierce* if it appears that parental decisions will jeopardize the health or safety of the child, or have a potential for significant social burdens.[35]

Earlier in his opinion, the chief justice noted that although Jefferson emphasized the need for *education* as a bulwark of a free people against tyranny, there is nothing to indicate he had in mind compulsory *schooling* through any fixed age beyond a basic grade. Even more encouraging are his words last quoted, which suggest that parental decisions must prevail unless the government can show that the parents have jeopardized the health and safety of the child or have created a potential for significant social burdens. Perhaps most significant of all of the chief justice's comments concerning the Amish is his remark, "Even their idiosyncratic separateness exemplifies the diversity we profess to admire and encourage."[36] Hence, it is not merely wishful thinking to conclude that the present Supreme Court has not committed itself to governmental domination in the schools. The actual result of the *Yoder* case speaks plainer than the opinion.

So long as the court maintains that parents are constitutionally assured the primary role in the upbringing of their children, any attempt by a government-created educationist establishment to diminish that role remains subject to challenge before our highest court. In nearly every instance, when the court has been confronted with governmental trespasses against that role, individual liberty has been vindicated. But the court has never candidly considered in its entirety the impact upon individual liberty of an educationist establishment that enlists the aid of government to force ever increasing tax loads for its support, that attempts to use the power of government to standardize schooling for the primary benefit of government-employed educationists, or other special interests, and that, in combination therewith, invokes the further power of government to fine or imprison recalcitrants.

In an opinion that many regard as the finest expression in this century of our abiding concern for individual freedom, Justice Jackson stated principles that may well point to eventual freedom of choice for all Americans whose funds before school taxes would be sufficient to pay for non-governmental schooling:

> Without promise of a limiting Bill of Rights it is doubtful if our Constitution could have mustered enough strength to enable its ratification. To enforce those rights today is not to choose weak government over strong government. It is only to adhere as a means of strength to individual freedom of mind in preference to officially disciplined uniformity for which history indicates a disappointing and disastrous end.[37]

> The very purpose of a Bill of Rights was to withdraw certain subjects from the vicissitudes of political controversy, to place them beyond the reach of majorities and officials and to establish them as legal principles to be applied by the courts. One's right to life, liberty, and property, to free speech, a free press, freedom of worship and assembly, and other fundamental rights may not be sub-

mitted to vote; they depend on the outcome of no elections.[38]

If there is any fixed star in our constitutional constellation, it is that no official, high or petty, can prescribe what shall be orthodox in politics, nationalism, religion, or other matters of opinion or force citizens to confess by word or act their faith therein. If there are any circumstances which permit an exception, they do not now occur to us.[39]

Justice Jackson was fully aware of the problems inherent in the court's attempt to pigeonhole schooling as either secular or sectarian, and his forecast of impending difficulties has proved accurate:

Our public school, if not a product of Protestantism, at least is more consistent with it than with the Catholic culture and scheme of values. It is a relatively recent development dating from about 1840. It is organized on the premises that secular education can be isolated from all religious teaching so that the school can inculcate all needed temporal knowledge and also maintain a strict and lofty neutrality as to religion. The assumption is that after the individual has been instructed in worldly wisdom he will be better fitted to choose his religion. Whether such a disjunction is possible, and if possible whether it is wise, are questions I need not try to answer.[40]

It seems to me that to do so is to allow zeal for our own ideas of what is good in public instruction to induce us to accept the role of a super board of education for every school district in the nation....It is idle to pretend that this task is one for which we can find in the Constitution one word to help us as judges to decide where the secular ends and the sectarian begins in education. Nor can we find guidance in any other legal source. It is a matter on which we can find no law but our own prepossessions.[41]

Relying first on the guarantee of liberty in the Fourteenth Amendment, and later on the religion and

speech clauses of the First Amendment, the Supreme
Court has, without significant exception, ruled against
regimentation of the content of schooling by state and
local officials by invalidating all such efforts, including
the prohibition of foreign language instruction (*Meyer v.
Nebraska*), compulsory attendance at public schools only
(*Pierce v. Society of Sisters*), detailed public approval of
private school curriculum and teachers (*Farrington v.
Tokushige*), the use of public school property for the
conduct of religious services during school hours (*Mc-
Collum v. Board of Education*, 333 U.S. 203), proscrip-
tions against the teaching of evolution (*Epperson v.
Arkansas*), official prayers for public schools (*Engel v.
Vitale*)[42], and prohibitions against the wearing of black
arm bands by students protesting the Vietnam War
(*Tinker v. Des Moines*, 393 U.S. 503).[43] Finally, in the
Yoder case, the court held that Wisconsin's interest in
compulsory schooling was outweighed by the right of
Amish parents to conduct their children's education in
accordance with their religious traditions, after the children had passed the eighth grade. Thus, when consideration is given only to the results in such cases, it can be
concluded that compulsory schooling has not enjoyed a
friendly reception from the Supreme Court thus far.

Misgivings do arise when attention is paid to some of
the language in the court's opinions, such as its repeated
references to the legitimate, but never defined, interest
of government in an "educated" citizenry, or its unsup-
portable categorization of all schooling as either secular
or religious. If the Supreme Court should ever attempt
to specify the minimum content of that "education" that
would satisfy the legitimate interests of government, it
will have assumed prerogatives that no court, or any
other agency of government, should possess in a free so-

ciety. In that event the court's distinction between the secular and the sectarian would prove of no real value, for the problems presented in dealing with the appropriate content of schooling are as complex, as profound, and as unlimited as the meaning of life itself. Any attempt to establish by law uniformity in curriculum for minors or in their teachers' qualifications, necessarily rests on the proposition that the child is the creature of the state. Traditionally, government has intervened in the parent-child relationship only when the welfare of the child has been jeopardized in some particular instance by demonstrable parental neglect. In keeping with this tradition, it is suggested here that the government may constitutionally interfere with parental control of education only when, in a specific case, the government is prepared to prove that the parents' responsibility for the education of their children has either been abandoned or is being exercised so as to damage the wellbeing of the child. Courts *are* equipped to deal with such problems on a case-by-case basis, and they have no pecuniary interest in attempting to ignore individual differences by formulating uniform requirements as to curriculum content or teaching qualifications. Much of what the Supreme Court has said is consistent with this suggested limited role for government as the counselor of children under the Constitution. It would seem to be the only approach that minimizes the inherent contradictions between government compulsion in schooling and the individual parent's primary right and duty to shape the destiny of his children while they are immature.

For the great majority of Americans, however, both the right to choose a nongovernmental school for their children and the correlative right to pursue that course free from official disciplined uniformity, have become meaningless, notwithstanding that the Supreme Court has said that these rights are fundamental under the Constitution. This will continue to be true as long as government is not required to account to the taxpaying parent for that portion of his school tax bill that is attributable to the cost of schooling his children, so that he may decide whether that part of his resources available for educational purposes will be used for governmental or for independent schooling. Until that issue is resolved in favor of freedom of educational choice, most parents will have to continue to submit the minds of their children to the government-standardized courses provided by public schools. The present state of the law makes it impossible for them to do otherwise.

NOTES

[1]*Pierce v. Society of Sisters,* 268 U.S. 510.

[2]*Lemon v. Kurtzman,* 403 U.S. 602, 621.

[3]*Murdock v. Pennsylvania,* 319 U.S. 105, 113.

[4]*Ibid.,* 112.

[5]*Lynch v. Hosehold Finance,* 405 U.S. 538.

[6]*Abington School District v. Schempp,* 347 U.S. 203, 242.

[7]*Murdock v. Pennsylvania,* 319 U.S. 105, 115.

[8]*Lemon v. Kurtzman,* 403 U.S. 602, 641.

[9]Murdock v. Pennsylvania, 319 U.S. 109, 11.

[10]*Sloan v. Lemon,* _____ U.S. _____, 37 L.Ed.2d 939.

[11]*Levitt v. Committee for Public Education,* _____ U.S. _____, 37 L.Ed.2d 736.

[12]*Nyquist v. Committee for Public Education,* _____ U.S. _____, 37 L.Ed.2d 948.

[13]*Walz v. Tax Commission,* 397 U.S. 664.

[14]*San Antonio School District v. Rodriguez,* _____ U.S. _____, 36 L.Ed.2d 16.

[15]*Board of Education v. Allen,* 392 U.S. 236, 244.

[16]*Ibid.,* 260.

[17]*Ibid.,* 256.

[18]*Ibid.,* 264.

[19]*Epperson v. Arkansas,* 393 U.S. 97, 114.

[20]*Lemon v. Kurtzman,* 403 U.S. 602, 617.

[21]*Abington School District v. Schempp,* 374 U.S. 203, 226.

[22]*Wisconsin Industrial School for Girls v. Clark County,* 103 Wis. 651, 655.

[23]*Lemon v. Kurtzman,* 403 U.S. 602, 624.

[24]John Dewey, *A Common Faith* (New Haven: Yale University Press, 1934), 86.

[25]*Ibid.,* 87.

[26]John Gardner, *Towards A Truly Public Education* (New York: Myrin Institute Inc., Vol. 18, Winter, 1965-1966), 25.

[27]*Welsh v. United States,* 398 U.S. 333, 343.

[28]Pierce v. Society of Sisters, 268 U.S. 510, 534-35.

[29]*Meyer v. Nebraska,* 262 U.S. 390, 401-2.

[30]*Farrington v. Tokushige,* 273 U.S. 284, 293-4.

[31]*Ibid.,* 298.

[32]*Cheney Bros. v. Doris Silk Corp.,* 2 Cir., 35 F.2d 279, 280.

[33]Wisconsin v. Yoder, 406 U.S. 205.

[34]*Ibid.*

[35]*Ibid.*

[36]*Ibid.*

[37]*West Virginia State Bd. of Education v. Barnette,* 319 U.S. 624, 636-37.

[38]*Ibid.,* 638.

[39]*Ibid.,* 642.

[40]*Everson v. Board of Education,* 330 U.S. 1, 23-24.

[41]*McCollum v. Board of Education,* 333 U.S. 203, 237-38.

[42]*Engel v. Vitale,* 370 U.S. 421.

[43]*Tinker v. Des Moines,* 393 U.S. 503.

We turn now to compulsion as imposed by the several states. Attorney Robert P. Baker explores the limits of educational variety permitted in various locales, with special emphasis on the right of parents to educate their offspring at home, and the right of parents to withdraw their children from public school courses they deem immoral or objectionable.

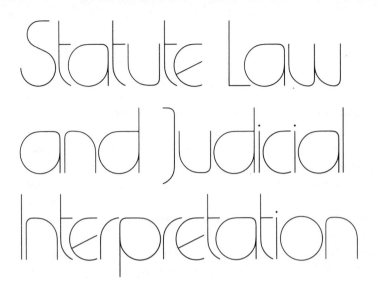

Statute Law and Judicial Interpretation

Robert P. Baker

The subject of schooling is not mentioned in the United States Constitution and there is no right to be educated recognized therein. Under the Ninth and Tenth Amendments, schooling is a matter left to the people and to the several states. As the Supreme Court of the United States put it in a case decided seventy-three years ago:

> The education of the people in schools maintained by state taxation is a matter belonging to the respective states, and any interference on the part of federal author-

ity with the management of such schools cannot be justified except in the case of a clear and unmistakable
disregard of rights secured by the supreme law of the
land.[1]

The nexus of federal and state law regarding schooling does not emerge unless and until two circumstances
exist concurrently: one, the individual state does in fact
maintain a tax-supported school system, and, two, the
laws governing that system infringe upon some right
guaranteed by the United States Constitution. When
James Meredith entered the University of Mississippi accompanied by federal marshals, the right being enforced
was not Mr. Meredith's right to schooling; neither he
nor anyone else has any right to be schooled at the expense of the Mississippi taxpayers. What Mr. Meredith
did have a right to, as a citizen of the United States, was
equality of treatment under the laws of Mississippi, regardless of the subject of those laws. If, in order to
thwart him, the State of Mississippi had exercised its
right to abolish its public schools, Mr. Meredith would
have had no remedy in the federal courts.

The question often arises in popular discussion whether a state may, consonant with the Constitution, compel
parents to educate their children. Despite a widespread
belief to the contrary, the Supreme Court of the United
States has never directly answered this question. Unfortunately, however, any productive discussion of the merits has been foreclosed by the court's intimating what it
would have decided, had it been presented with the
question. The popular belief arose out of the famous
1925 case concerning an Oregon school law that required all children to be given instruction solely in public schools. The United States Supreme Court struck
down this law, pointing out that

> The fundamental theory of liberty upon which all govern-
> ments in this Union repose excludes any general power of
> the state to standardize its children by forcing them to
> accept instruction from public teachers only.[2]

Thus far and no further, fine. But on the preceding
page of the court's opinion, in a mere dictum, a judicial
aside, Mr. Justice McReynolds also mentioned the fact
that the case presented no question

> concerning the power of the state reasonably to regulate
> all schools, to inspect, supervise, and examine them, their
> teachers and pupils; to require that all children of proper
> age attend some school, that teachers shall be of good
> moral character and patriotic disposition, that certain
> studies plainly essential to good citizenship must be
> taught, and that nothing be taught which is manifestly in-
> imical to the public welfare.[3]

Mr. Justice McReynolds was absolutely right. The case
presented no such questions. It is a mystery to me why
he found it necessary to unburden himself of these legally irrelevant observations. In the years since this case,
Pierce v. Society of Sisters, was decided, many state courts
have seized upon it avidly, citing the McReynolds dictum
as if it were a judicial holding, in order to justify the
most outrageous infringements upon the rights of children and their parents. It has been employed to support
the proposition that parents may be compelled to educate their children, and moreover, may be compelled to
educate them in accordance with state-prescribed curricula taught by state-approved teachers. The *Pierce* case,
so widely regarded as a victory for civil liberties, in fact
did enormous damage. Properly construed, it established
only one point: that private schools have a constitutional
right to exist.

I will return to the constitutional implications of compulsory schooling laws when I discuss how they tend to function in practice, but at this point I want to go into the content of the laws and classify them. Two preliminaries: First, it should be remembered that, under the common law emerging case by case over the last nine centuries, the courts uniformly held that no offense was committed by a parent who failed to provide for his children's education. Our jurisprudence has always held that a father has a moral duty to educate, but not a legal one, and a neglected child's prayer for remedy must be directed to God rather than to the king. Consequently, every compulsory schooling law derives from statute, from specific legislative enactment. This is one of the areas in which there does not exist any law until a statute has been passed. Moreover, every compulsory schooling statute is penal in nature: it forbids certain acts and omissions, providing for criminal penalties in the event of disobedience. Secondly, it must be remembered that when the word "law" is used in this context, it signifies not only the bare words of the legislation as found in the statute books, but in addition the holdings of the courts as they have construed the legislation in cases arising under it. The words of the statute are but half the law; what the courts say those words mean in practice is the other half.

Since there are fifty jurisdictions in the United States, you might at first think we are confronted with an unmanageable multitude of dozens of different laws. In broad outline, however, the laws bear certain similarities, and I have found it useful in my studies to classify compulsory schooling laws under two headings deriving from the social attitudes behind them. I have labeled these classifications, perhaps whimsically but I think accurately, the "other guy" type of compulsory schooling law and the "cookie-cutter" type.

The argument underlying the first type of statute runs as follows: "My colleague who favors the compulsory schooling law stoutly maintains that he would of course educate his children even in the absence of the law, and he admits that I share his sense of moral obligation and would also provide for my children's education without a gun being held to my head. But don't you see—there is that fellow across the street, or if it turns out that the fellow across the street is in fact educating his children, then there is that fellow down the block or in the next county or *somewhere* there is *somebody* who, if there were no compulsory schooling law, would not educate his kids. And thus it follows with impeccable logic that laws prescribing the schooling of millions of youngsters are essential if an entire generation of illiterates is to be avoided." I have yet to meet the man who will admit to me that if it were not for the law, he would leave his children in ignorance; it is for that "other guy" who is so derelict in his parental duties, and whom I have never encountered, that we need the law.

Despite the manifest absurdity of the "other guy" argument, it has important practical consequences for the law. Where adopted, it results in laws that require, on their face at least, no more than what most parents would do anyway. In its naked and minimal form, the statute underlying such a law might read thus:

> Every person having custody of a minor child between the ages of 8 and 16 years shall cause such child to attend upon instruction in the public schools of this state, or in a private school, or shall cause such child to be otherwise equivalently instructed.

The significant aspect of such a statute, which of course, is always amplified by sections detailing qualifications of students, curriculum content, periods of attendance, and similar minutiae, is this phrase "otherwise equivalently instructed." So the statutes read in New York, New Jersey and Ohio. These legislatures have done no more than to enjoin all those other guys to afford their children an education substantially as good as that given in the public schools. How they do so is, on the face of the statute, no concern of the legislature.

It can be reasonably argued, I think, that the "other guy" type of compulsory schooling law, while objectionable in terms of liberty, is at least tolerable under any practical circumstances that are likely to arise in a free society. It may overlap laws regarding child abuse; it may indeed be superfluous in a community where the value of education is universally recognized; it is certain to be unavailing against that one parent in a million to whom it might be applied in practice. But it can be lived with.

I now turn to the second class of compulsory schooling law, engendered by a conceptually distinct social attitude, and certainly more conducive to oppressive law. It was advanced openly during the later nineteenth and early twentieth centuries, and while much muted today nevertheless lies behind the compulsory schooling laws of many American jurisdictions. We are all familiar with the myth of the melting pot, which, in its educational manifestation, extolled the virtue of taking the children of the newly arrived immigrants, this wretched refuse of some teeming shore, and processing them through the public school cookie-cutter, turning out millions of standardized Americans. If the immigrant youngsters happened to acquire some intellectual attainments along the way, so much the better, but the fundamental purpose of the public school system, under the "cookie-cutter" theory, was their Americanization.

Now what kind of law would we expect to evolve from the cookie-cutter theory? Obviously, a law intolerant of any deviation from the norm, requiring strict supervision of the entire educational process, culturally stultifying, and only grudgingly permitting private schooling to exist. *Pierce v. Society of Sisters*, for example, arose out of the determination of the Oregon legislature to assimilate the children of the foreign-born, particularly those treacherous Germans. In order to accomplish this, it was clear that the Catholic and Lutheran parochial schools had to be destroyed, and it was the purpose of the law to do just that. The "cookie-cutter" approach was also responsible for those laws passed in Iowa, Kansas, and Nebraska in the early 1920s requiring that all instruction in any school be conducted solely in the English language and moreover forbidding the teaching of any foreign language in the elementary grades.

Now having made clear, I hope, the conceptual distinctions between the two major classes of compulsory schooling law, we can sharpen our language somewhat. The concept of "compulsory" education (as distinct from schooling) is absurd. In reality, the laws can do no more than compel the custodian of a child to expose him to a reasonable amount and kind of instruction, in the case of an "other guy" type law, or, in the case of a "cookie-cutter" law, to enroll him in and ensure his attendance at an approved institution.

Let us now examine the functioning of particular laws in each of these two major classes as exemplified in a number of contrasting cases. For more than twenty-five years, the New Jersey compulsory schooling statute has contained wording identical to that I gave you earlier, that is, a clause permitting "equivalent instruction elsewhere than at school." When Mr. and Mrs. Bongart were accused of being disorderly persons in 1937 because they themselves were educating their children in their home, it might have appeared that the prosecution had no case—at least if the defendants could prove equivalence of instruction. In convicting them, however, the trial judge said,

> I cannot conceive how a child can receive in the home instruction and experiences in group activity and in social outlook in any manner or form comparable to that provided in the public school.[4]

When the defendant father protested that "I am not interested in method, but in results," the judged replied,

> ...that theory is archaic, mechanical, and destructive of the finer instincts of the child. It does seem to me, too, quite unlikely that this type of instruction could produce a child with all the attributes that a person of education, refinement, and character should possess.[5]

We see in this case an obvious example of the "cookie-cutter" theory in practice, superimposed by judicial fiat, and an illustration of my earlier comment that the statute is but half the law.

An even more outrageous case, *Knox v. O'Brien*, arose under the same New Jersey statute in 1950. Therein it was proved at the trial that the mother, who was instructing her children at home, held a state teacher's certificate, and that the children were taught state-prescribed subjects, from state-approved textbooks, during the usual public school hours. Nevertheless, the court clung to the "cookie-cutter" approach, asserting that

> Free association with other children being denied to Mark and Eileen, by design or otherwise, which is afforded

them at public school, leads...to the conclusion that they are not receiving education equivalent to that provided in the public schools.[6]

The court's use of the phrase "by design or otherwise" reveals the irony of the case, since it was precisely in order to avoid forced association with other children, children whom the O'Briens considered an immoral influence, that they withdrew their own youngsters from the public schools.

We can see, in light of these two cases, that for many years New Jersey in fact had a compulsory school attendance law. At last, in 1967, a case involving home instruction came before a judge who had the insight to ask what is in retrospect a rather obvious question: If the legislature had indeed intended that education be imparted only in a group, that is, in a "school," then why did it frame a statute providing for an alternative to school? The court then ruled that New Jersey law requires nothing more than a showing of academic equivalence and acquitted the parents who were educating their child at home. In the seven years since this case, *State v. Massa*,[7] New Jersey has had a pure "other guy" type of compulsory education law.

It is not always the judges, of course, who try to ram their "cookie-cutter" philosophy down their neighbors' throats. In Kansas, for example, in 1965, one legislator secured the passage of a bill repealing the exemption from the compulsory education law which had been granted to children who, regardless of age, had completed the eighth grade. The bill was intended, in the legislator's own words, "to force the Amish into the mainstream of American life," and provided that all children below the age of sixteen were required to attend an approved school, regardless of previous educational attainment. I will explore the peculiar difficulties that the laws have visited upon the Amish in more depth when we analyze constitutional problems in greater detail; for now, let me merely assure you that before attempting to force an Amishman to do anything, I would sooner chew on rocks. The Amish community did attempt to comply with the new law to the greatest extent possible, consonant with their religious convictions proscribing worldly learning beyond that normally acquired in elementary school. They established their own school, taught by an Amishman, wherein courses in agronomy, animal husbandry, domestic arts, and similar subjects were offered. Shortly thereafter, Leroy Garber, father of one of the children in the Amish school, was prosecuted under the new law and convicted. This conviction was sustained by the Kansas Supreme Court, which held that the Amish school, since it was not conducted by a state-certified teacher and did not follow the same curriculum as that presented in the public high schools, was merely "programmed home instruction," and consequently not permissible, even if demonstrably equivalent education was imparted, because the Kansas compulsory schooling statute made no provision for instruction outside an approved school.[8] Kansas, it can be seen, has a compulsory school attendance law. In the face of continued resistance by the Amish, the "mainstream" amendment was at last repealed and the previous exemption restored to the law. But this came too late for Leroy Garber. By the time the United States Supreme Court denied his final appeal, he had another child approaching completion of elementary school, and could not face a repetition of his ordeal. Garber sold his farm and moved away from Kansas, hoping to find that religious liberty in search of which his ancestors had em-

igrated to America more than two hundred years before.

States other than Kansas have statutes which do not
specifically permit compliance by education outside a
conventional school. But where the courts are genuinely
concerned with education and reject the "cookie-cutter"
approach, results apparently contrary to the strict wording of such statutes have been encountered. In the Illinois case of *People v. Levisen*, for example, in 1950, a
young girl was being educated at home by her parents,
devout Seventh-day Adventists, who believed that educating her in a conventional school in competition with
other children would instill an un-Christian pugnacity of
character. They decried the fact that faith in the Bible
could not be taught in a conventional school, and contended, in their words, that

> for the first eight or ten years of a child's life, the field or
> garden is the best schoolroom, the mother the best teach-
> er, and nature the best lesson book.[9]

There was no question that the intellectual atmosphere
of the Levisen home was quite good; the father was a
college graduate, and the mother had two years of college training, including work in pedagogy and educational psychology. The child's educational program was
guided by a church correspondence course, with regular
daily hours for instruction, recitation and study. Whatever the abstract merits of the parents' educational philosophy, their practice was apparently beneficial to their
child, since upon examination using standard tests she
showed a proficiency comparable to the average third
grade student, although she was only seven years old.
All of this notwithstanding, the parents were convicted
in the trial court for violating what was, on its face, a

compulsory school attendance statute. The conviction was appealed, both the prosecution and the defendants agreeing in their belief that the Levisen child was not attending a private school, which, under the wording of the statute, was the only permissible alternative to public school. But judicial interpretation, of which we have already mentioned several examples, is a sword that cuts more than one way, and the Illinois Supreme Court, in reversing the conviction of the Levisens, held that the alleged fact agreed upon by the parties was actually a conclusion of law, to be decided upon by the court, and that the Levisens, contrary to their concession to the prosecutor, were operating a "private school" within the intention of the legislature. The Illinois courts have been unusually wise and perceptive in regard to compulsory schooling, and their attitude is well exemplified in a 1966 decision upholding Chicago's experimental dual-enrollment plan, under which parents may comply with the law by having their children attend public school for part of the day and another educational institution of the parent's choice for the remainder. The *Levisen* court formulated the "other guy" philosophy in its least objectionable form when it observed that

> The law is not made to punish parents who provide their children with instruction equal or superior to that obtainable in the public schools. It is made for the parent who fails or refuses to properly educate his child.[10]

The most tragic case I have encountered in my studies illustrates the "cookie-cutter" theory at its most virulent and oppressive. Following the conviction of her parents for violating the compulsory school attendance law of the State of Washington in 1959, a young girl was adjudged delinquent and dependent, and an order was entered making her a ward of the court. It is not clear what the judge's actual motive may have been for taking such drastic action, but the practical effect of the order was to make her removal from the state unlawful without the court's consent. Her parents' religious convictions forbade attendance at a conventional school, and they had been educating her at home. The trial court found as a fact that the parents' religious liberty was indeed infringed by the requirement of school attendance and further found as a fact that the instruction being imparted to the girl in her home was at least the academic equivalent of that available in the public schools. The Washington statute contains no provision permitting instruction elsewhere than in a public or private school. Although the trial court, as later events showed, was sympathetic, it did not, at the time of trial, indulge in the fiction employed by the Illinois Supreme Court in the *Levisen* case five years earlier. Physical custody of the child was left in the parents, conditioned upon their providing for her education in conformity with state law.

Subsequent to the entry of his order of wardship, however, the trial judge researched the matter more deeply and discovered that the Washington legislature had never promulgated any standards governing private schools. Having found this happy means of squaring the law with the justice of the case, the trial judge promptly reversed himself, ruling that in light of the adequacy of the instruction being given the child in her home, she was in fact attending a "private school."

The state's attorney appealed, and in an incredible decision, by a five to four vote, the Washington Supreme Court held that, in spite of the absence of any legislative standards for private schools and in spite of the indisputably proper education being afforded the child, no school could be deemed to exist unless instruction were being given by a teacher certified by the state of Washington. The lower court's original order was reinstated. To their credit, the four dissenters wrote a blistering minority opinion, pointing out that it was the function of the lower court to determine what was in the best interests of the child and that it had done so. I submit to you that this case, *Shoreline v. Superior Court,* is a disgrace to American jurisprudence.[11]

Having shown the functioning of the compulsory schooling laws in these relatively simple cases, I want now to consider some of the subtler details of these laws that give rise to greater complexity, in particular the constitutional implications of the regulations embodied in most compulsory schooling laws regarding religion, health, race, and curriculum. In the typical compulsory schooling dispute, a parent fails or refuses to send his child to school, or, in those jurisdictions permitting it, to provide equivalent instruction. Very often such failure is based upon the religious-moral or educational-social convictions of the parent, and when prosecuted, the defendant relies upon an alleged violation of his constitutional rights.

Consider the famous case of *West Virginia State Board of Education v. Barnette,*[12] wherein the constitutionality of a mandatory flag salute was considered. Barnette was a Jehovah's Witness, and for reasons deemed sufficient and compelling by them, Jehovah's Witnesses will not render any form of obeisance whatsoever to any tangible object, including a flag. Embodied in the West Virginia school law was a commandment that every child attending the public schools should salute the flag of the United States each morning. Refusal was considered insubordination. Couple these considerations with a compulsory school attendance law and it is obvious that strife is inevitable. Either their parents removed them from the schools, or, in many instances, the children of the Jehovah's Witnesses were expelled and threatened with terms in a reformatory for criminally inclined juveniles. Their parents were prosecuted, both for violation of the compulsory schooling law and for causing delinquency of minors. Their defense, of course, was that the flag salute law violated their religious liberty, guaranteed by the First Amendment to the United States Constitution.

The Supreme Court of the United States did strike down the West Virginia law, but it is interesting to note that its reasoning was not grounded primarily upon the infringement of religious liberty that the law entailed. Rather, the court made it clear that the First Amendment's guarantee of free speech was sufficient to decide the matter:

> It is also to be noted that the compulsory flag salute and pledge requires affirmation of a belief and an attitude of mind . . . . To sustain the compulsory flag salute we are required to say that a Bill of Rights which guards the individual's right to speak his own mind, left it open to public authorities to compel him to utter what is not in his mind.[13]

That might seem to have settled the matter conclusively, but as recently as 1966 members of another minority sect—in this case, Black Muslims—had to struggle up to the New Jersey Supreme Court before their right not to salute the flag was reaffirmed. This despite the fact that the New Jersey school regulations regarding flag saluting specifically exempt from its provisions those having conscientious scruples which would thereby be offended! The significance of the United States Supreme Court's opinion in *Barnette*, emphasizing the free speech aspects of the right not to salute, can be seen in the fact that the local school board that had expelled the recalcitrants defended its action on the specious grounds that the Black Muslims' objections to saluting were based as much upon their political beliefs as upon their religious beliefs. Of course, it makes no difference.

More strictly pertinent to the First Amendment's protection of religious liberty are those cases involving the conflict between compulsory schooling laws and Bible-reading or prayer in the schools. Until very recently, such conflicts were frequently the objects of litigation in our courts. The earliest so-called public schools were in fact Protestant schools supported by taxation, and part of their efforts to inculcate true Christianity in the young consisted of the reading of the King James Bible and the recitation of Protestant-oriented prayers. This practice continues even today, in defiance of the rulings of the United States Supreme Court. While children are no longer being expelled for their refusal to participate in exercises repugnant to their religious beliefs, or if they are, the cases have not reached the courts, this was once a common occurrence, and—at the risk of some degree of digression—I think that it would be good to examine this matter not only because of its peripheral relationship to compulsory schooling problems, but in order to clarify some of the legal issues surrounding prayer in the schools. The now famous case of *Engel v. Vitale*[14] arose in New York. The regents of that state, who are invested with broad and general supervisory powers over the operation of the public schools, published, in the early 1960s, a *Statement on Moral and Spiritual Training in the Schools*, saying that

We believe that this statement will be subscribed to by all

men and women of good will, and we call upon all of them to aid in giving life to our program.[15]

Embodied in the *Statement* was a short prayer, composed by the regents themselves, to be recited at the beginning of each school day. This order was issued by local school boards and did contain a provision permitting any child who so desired to absent himself during the recitation. The prayer itself went as follows:

> Almighty God, we acknowledge our dependence upon Thee, and we beg Thy blessings upon us, our teachers, and our country.

A substantial number of New York parents objected to this practice, and ten of them brought suit in the state courts to have it enjoined as a violation of the First Amendment. The New York Court of Appeals, while acknowledging that the prayer was offensive to Unitarians, Jews and Ethical Culturists, nevertheless denied the parents their requested injunction. Since a federal question was involved, the United States Supreme Court accepted their appeal, and in a 6-1 decision unleashed a continuing controversy by holding that the required prayer recitation is indeed violative of the Constitution.

It is important here to appreciate precisely what the Supreme Court said—and perhaps even more important to appreciate what it did not say. There is no legal ban upon children praying in school or anywhere else. There are no U.S. marshals stationed in classrooms waiting to swoop down on any youngsters caught looking heavenward and moving their lips. The recent proposed amendment to the Constitution, allegedly designed to guarantee children the right to pray, was not only a political smokescreen but redundant: my child's right to pray, in or out of school, is already protected by that same First Amendment that protects him from having prayers thrust upon him by public officials. What the Supreme Court did say and, when we get to the heart of the matter, all that it said, is that it is no business of the government to be composing or prescribing any prayers for anybody, directly or indirectly. Honest confusion on this issue—not the confusion which has been deliberately fomented by some congressmen—is perhaps understandable, since even Mr. Justice Stewart, the lone dissenter and a jurist for whom I have a great deal of respect, failed to grasp the essential point of the court's opinion. He said, in part:

> I think that to deny the wish of these school children to join in reciting this prayer is to deny them the opportunity of sharing in the spiritual heritage of our nation.[16]

Everyone should agree that if any child were denied his right to pray it would indeed be a monstrous injustice and contrary to our constitutional principles. No such denial is remotely implied in the decision on the New York Regents' case.

This short excursion into the school prayer controversy is not wholly unrelated to compulsory schooling questions. Not only do we see an attempt to use the schools for unrelated social objectives, but there have been direct conflicts involving compulsory education and religious exercises. Since these exercises are considered part of the curriculum, the courts have generally dealt with them in terms of the parents' right to reject certain courses of study for their child. Parents have voiced the most unusual objections. I have found parents rejecting such apparently innocuous things as grammar, algebra, and domestic science. One fellow fought all the way to the Supreme Court of Indiana in order to avoid submitting his daughter to the study of singing. Almost without exception, the courts in this country have been sympathetic in regard to parental objections. As the Supreme Court of Oklahoma put it in 1957, reaffirming a well established legal doctrine in that state:

> The parent...has a right to make a reasonable selection from the prescribed course of study for his child to pursue, and this selection must be respected by the school authorities, as the right of the parent in that regard is superior to that of the school officers and the teachers.[17]

The school law of New York specifically exempts the children of Christian Scientists, who reject the received wisdom in regard to health and disease, from the study of hygiene. In signing the bill granting the exemption, the governor of New York stated:

> I believe it to be a simple fundamental of freedom of religion that the state shall compel no child to learn principles clearly contrary to the basic tenets of his religious faith.[18]

There may well be a fallacy involved here, since there are very few young children who can be said to have a religious faith in the usual sense of that concept, and in fact it is their parents' religious sensibilities that the law is solicitous of. But this statement exemplifies the current attitude. The sole exception to the courts' libertarian approach to curriculum choice, as suggested earlier, concerns, or until the recent prayer and Bible-reading decisions muted the conflicts, did concern religious exercises. As late as 1955, the Massachusetts Supreme Court, in affirming the conviction of Buddhist parents who were offended when their child was required to participate in Bible-reading, held that this was no defense to a charge of violating the compulsory education law by keeping the child at home. But even in this area, a minority of courts have defended parental curriculum choice. In a case arising out of a parental request to have a child exempted from religious exercises, the Supreme Court of Colorado wrote a ringing defense of individual rights, saying that

> the right of parents to have their children taught where, when, how, what and by whom they may judge best, are [sic] among the liberties guaranteed by section 1 of the Fourteenth Amendment of the United States Constitution....The parent has a constitutional right to have his children educated in the public schools of the state...and to direct, within limits, his children's studies. The school board, though with full power to prescribe the studies, cannot make the surrender of the second a condition...of the first. They cannot say to him, "you have a constitutional right to deny your child the study of biology, and you have a constitutional right to have him taught in the public schools, but, if you are admitted to the latter, we shall deny you the former."[19]

In sharp contrast to the manner in which the compulsory schooling laws have been applied in regard to curricular choice is their application when parents have sought regular absences, for entire days. In Pennsylvania, Muslim parents kept their child from school every Friday, a day revered by Islam and analogous to the Judeo-Christian sabbath. In affirming their conviction, the court held that, while the parents might send their child to a school that recognized their holy day, so long as the child was enrolled in a public school he would have to adhere to its schedule, and there was no right to conform to the compulsory schooling statute only part of the time.[20] So too in a case in 1954 that had no religious implications. Therein a young girl, whose exceptional talent was freely acknowledged, left school every

Wednesday afternoon for ballet lessons. The court held that it was not permissible to interrupt the regular course of study, and her father was convicted of violating the compulsory schooling law.[21]

The general rule then, throughout the country, at least in those states having the relatively mild "other guy" type of law, is that you can get your child exempted from specific courses of study, but you may not take regular chunks of time out of the public school schedule.

There are many citizens who, usually on religious grounds, differ from the overwhelming majority in regard to matters of health and disease. In particular, their religious beliefs forbid inoculations. Perhaps they know something, since I recently read a news item stating that the Public Health Service has reversed its previous stance and will now advise against routine smallpox vaccination. Be that as it may, you can easily see that coupling compulsory attendance laws with regulations making vaccination a precondition for school enrollment is going to make lawyers rich, even if it accomplishes no good for anyone else. The uniform rule of law today, in every jurisdiction that has passed upon the question, is, that where inoculation is a precondition to school attendance, refusal to have your child inoculated is the legal equivalent of refusal to cause him to attend school, and exposes you to prosecution under the compulsory schooling law. Many states have grafted exemptions onto their school laws, providing for children of persons whose religious tenets would be violated by vaccination. Such is the case in New Jersey and North Carolina, for example. With the almost total eradication of smallpox and diphtheria in the United States, public health and school officials may well be abandoning their previous fanaticism in regard to inoculation of children, and disputes are, I presume, being adjusted on the local level. No such cases have reached the appellate courts in the last few years.

We could hardly quit the area wherein religious beliefs come into conflict with the compulsory schooling laws without mentioning, however superficially, the tribulations of the Amish people. The Amish, frequently called "the Plain People," are a sect deeply committed to their views of the Christian life. Their doctrines, and to a large extent their practices, have through choice been frozen as they were at the dawn of the seventeenth century. Over the centuries, the aloofness from the larger society around them that is the Amish practice has had a reciprocal effect of both preserving and of reinforcing their cultural distinctness. The Amish accept in theory and practice an injunction found in the twelfth chapter of *Romans*:

> Be not conformed to this world: but be ye transformed by the renewing of your mind, that ye may prove what *is* that good, and acceptable, and perfect will of God.

There are many Amish beliefs that have brought them into conflict with the larger society around them and its laws. They will not, for example, pay Social Security taxes, for does not St. Matthew tell us of Jesus's admonition in the Sermon on the Mount?

> Lay not up for yourselves treasures upon earth, where moth and rust doth corrupt, and where thieves break through and steal: But lay up for yourselves treasures in heaven. . . .

Not long ago the Amish were exempted from the payment of Social Security taxes, but previously, the agents of the I.R.S., undeterred by the scriptural allusions to thieves breaking through and stealing, have seized the property of Amishmen, selling it for pittances at public auction to satisfy assessments. As you might expect, the Amish are also thoroughgoing pacifists, and pushing them around demands just about as much courage as the average tax-collector possesses.

The doctrine that has brought the Amish into collision with compulsory schooling laws stems from the Dortricht Confession of 1632, which warned them against those who attend universities and, apparently in consequence, pervert the word of God. In practice, this doctrine has led the Amish to reject all "worldly" learning beyond that normally attained in the typical elementary school. It should be understood that the Amish are not opposed to learning *per se*. On the contrary, they stress literacy, so that their children may read the Bible, and they desire their children to be able to keep their accounts and to be fluent in liturgical German. Amish expertise in agronomy and animal husbandry is without equal. Since the Amish are predominantly farmers, the education they provide for their children when left in peace is quite adequate for the overwhelming majority who follow their forefathers' agrarian way of life. But it is often not sufficient to satisfy the requirements of compulsory schooling laws. This lack has nothing to do with the quality of education given Amish children. Compulsory schooling laws are not framed to take into account the qualitative—or for that matter even the quantitative—aspects of children's education. Rather, they all specify, without exception, that a child shall be exposed to instruction until he attains a certain age. This is administratively expedient, it is simple to the point of being simplistic, and it obviates any need to treat individuals individually. For most of us it makes no difference; for the Amish it does. What the Amish fear most is that their children, particularly teenagers, will be lured away from their culture by the temptations abounding in the modern consolidated school. It is a danger that the Amish will not tolerate, regardless of the penal sanctions involved, and short of capturing the Amish children physically—which has been done—there is little that governmental agencies have been able to do to force them into the public schools.

How then have the compulsory schooling laws functioned in this setting? Well, some states, trying to reach accommodation, have provided for exemptions. Pennsylvania, for example, once provided for permits to be issued to youngsters over the age of fifteen who were engaged in agricultural or domestic employment. The superintendent of public instruction, however, despite the fact that he was granted no discretion on the face of the pertinent statute, forbade the issuance of such permits without a showing of "dire need" on the part of the child's family. In practice, of course, this would result in an absolute denial of such permits to Amish youngsters, since no Amish family in "dire need" has ever been observed. The first test of the superintendent's usurpation came in a prosecution of an Amishman, whose permit application was denied, under the compulsory schooling law. His son had left school to help on the family farm. The court acquitted the defendant and held that the school regulations, as applied to the Amish, were unconstitutional. The prosecution's appeal was denied. Despite this setback, the school authorities continued to deny the permits that the Amish were entitled to under the law, and, six years later, were able to convince the court that it was a proper exercise of the superintendent's powers to place such conditions upon the issuance of them—no matter what the statute said.[22]

I think that one of the important points illustrated by this Pennsylvania experience is that it is dangerous, and often futile, for the legislature to enact a "tough" compulsory schooling law and then to graft exceptions onto it, relying upon public officials to carry out the purposes of the law in good faith. Where the persons who are to be benefited by the exception are politically weak, geographically concentrated, and easily identifiable, we may rely upon some officials to find ways of catering to local prejudices. Nor is it always mere prejudice that motivates local officials toward stringency in enforcing compulsory attendance laws against the Amish. Sometimes it is a matter of money. Most schools are supported by local property taxes, and the funds thus derived are supplemented, often in very large amounts relative to the amount raised locally, through additional monies voted out of the state treasury. The degree of this state aid, of course, is related directly to the average attendance in the schools seeking it.

The Wisconsin compulsory attendance statute reads, in part, as follows:

> § 118.15 *Compulsory school attendance* (1) (a) Unless the child has a legal excuse or has graduated from high school, any person having under his control a child who is between the ages of 7 and 16 years shall cause such child to attend school regularly during the full period and hours...that the public or private school in which such child should be enrolled is in session until the end of the school term...of the school year in which he becomes 16 years of age.

That sounds, so far, rather strict, a typical "cookie-cutter" statute, but skipping down to paragraph number four we find a provision that makes clear the reference to the child's possible legal excuse:

92813

> Instruction during the required period elsewhere than at
> school may be substituted for school attendance. Such in-
> struction must be approved by the department as substan-
> tially equivalent to instruction given to children of like
> ages in the public or private schools where such children
> reside.

So we can see that the legislature, by grafting an exemption clause onto an otherwise tough statute, has apparently converted it into an "other guy" statute concerned
only with seeing that children are in fact educated reasonably. We certainly would not expect conflict under it
to arise in regard to the Amish, who maintain their own
elementary schools.

The town of New Glarus, located in Green County,
about 75 miles west of Milwaukee, has a fine, modern
consolidated high school. The consolidated high school,
drawing its pupils from a much wider geographical area
and having a much larger physical plant than that char-
acterizing high schools of an earlier generation, is a continuing trend in American secondary education,
representing an attempt by school administrators to cope
with ever more pressing financial problems. New Glarus
is no exception, and—trying to look at the matter from
the viewpoint of local officials in good faith—we can see
that they must have been quite upset. Here were these
Amish families in Green County having youngsters who,
although they had completed their elementary education, were still below the age of sixteen and yet were not
attending the high school, thus in effect "depriving" that
school, and its pupils, of the increased state aid to which
it would otherwise have been entitled. The obvious solution? Enforce the law to its letter and compel the Amish
children to attend. I have alluded earlier to the absurdity of trying to compel the Amish to do anything against
their religious convictions. You have never seen passive

resistance until you have seen an Amishman with his back up, and thus the stage was set in Wisconsin for a repetition of those repressive acts, including what one high court judge has described as gestapo tactics, that have so outraged many of us in the past. But this time, in large part because of some brilliant legal talent enlisted in their behalf, the Amish were ultimately vindicated.

The lower court, which convicted three Amishmen whose children, though graduates of elementary school, were still under age 16, accepted as true the contention of the defense that enforcement of Wisconsin's compulsory attendance statute against the Amish violated their religious liberty under the First Amendment to the United States Constitution. But it went on to hold that such infringement was the necessary and justifiable consequence of a legitimate governmental policy, apparently relying in part upon a judicial distinction between religious beliefs absolutely guaranteed, and acts, which even if religiously motivated, are in all cases subject to regulation in the "public interest"—a distinction that originated almost a hundred years ago and has been undergoing judicial erosion ever since. The Supreme Court of Wisconsin, by a six to one decision, reversed these convictions, holding in accordance with a previous decision of the United States Supreme Court that, in order to justify an indirect infringement of a constitutional right, the state must show more than the fact that the offensive law furthers a legitimate governmental concern. As the chief justice of Wisconsin put it,

> A compelling interest is not just a general interest in the subject matter but the need to apply the regulation without exception to attain the purposes and objectives of the legislation. . . . To force a worldly education on all Amish

children, the majority of whom do not want or need it, in order to confer a dubious benefit on the few who might later reject their religion is not a compelling interest.

Since there was a question under the Constitution, the state of Wisconsin prosecuted a writ to the United States Supreme Court, which again held for the Amish. The majority opinion, by Chief Justice Burger, is not, in my judgment, an unmixed blessing; it contains a number of propositions that I believe are simply bad law and that open the door to invidious discrimination against non-religious dissenters or against those whose religious objections are not of long standing. A discussion of my misgivings, however, is beyond the scope of this presentation. Suffice it to say that, insofar as a Supreme Court decision can make them so, the Amish are safe.[23]

It is worth noting that the Wisconsin battle was needless. Today many states have managed to reach accommodations with the Amish. Pennsylvania, Indiana, Ohio, Iowa, and Maryland, for example, have provided in various ways for the Amish to satisfy the law by establishing vocational training plans for their under-sixteen children. Just such an accommodation was suggested to Wisconsin officials quite early in the course of this recent litigation, but was rejected by them on the grounds that the Amish children would not and could not thereby be afforded substantially equivalent "education."

The last aspect of the functioning of the compulsory schooling laws that must be covered relates to the consequences of violating them. You will have noticed, of course, such words as "prosecution" and "conviction," implying that violation of the compulsory schooling laws constitutes a criminal act. This is indeed true in every state of the Union. The precise nature of the crime consists of a failure or refusal to act. It is the recalcitrance of the child's custodian that is the essence of the offense. Nevertheless, it is possible to violate the law through a positive act in some states. Convictions have been sustained against those who, in the course of strikes or school boycotts, have urged parents to keep their children away from school or who have encouraged truancy in the pupils.

The courts have generally distinguished between the acts of the child and the omissions of the parents. For example, this distinction has been employed by sympathetic courts to resolve the flag-salute controversies mentioned earlier. If the *child* refuses to salute the flag, these courts have said, the criminal law may not as a matter of course impute this insubordination to the parents.

Several jurisdictions have held that the omission constituting the offense under the compulsory schooling laws must be accompanied by an intent to do wrong, a *mens rea* as the lawyers call it, amounting to wilfulness and defiance in order to sustain a conviction; but this is definitely a minority rule. In most states, violating the compulsory education law is on an evidentiary par with violating pure food laws. All the prosecution has to show is the statutory elements of the offense. Neither motive nor malice nor any other mental state matters.

Because compulsory schooling prosecutions so often arise out of circumstances peculiarly local, it is important to determine precisely where the crime occurs, and consequently where the accused is to be tried. The general rule is that the offense is committed where the child involved resides, not where he should have attended. Thus, if your child should have gone to a consolidated school thirty miles away, the jury that tries your case will nevertheless be composed of your neighbors.

Suppose you are educating your own child in some unconventional manner in a state having an "other guy" statute. Who has to prove what? It can make an enormous difference whether you have to prove that you come under some exception to the general rules, or the prosecutor has to prove that you don't. The general rule is that, where the compulsory schooling statute, in defining the offense against it, specifies several alternative modes of compliance, it is up to the prosecution to allege and prove non-compliance with each and every one of them. If, on the other hand, the statute prescribes a general rule, such as the very common provision "shall attend a public or private school," and then, separately, lists certain exceptions, all the prosecutor must do is allege your non-compliance with the general rule, while you must bring forth evidence in your defense that you come under one of the exceptions. Having produced some degree of evidence from which reasonable men could conclude that you do indeed come under some exception, you shift the burden back to the prosecution to prove that you don't, and, these being criminal charges, such proof must be beyond a reasonable doubt. You can see arising from these technical rules the reason for my earlier strictures against legislatures enacting tough "cookie-cutter" statutes, then tacking on exception clauses. The New York statute, for example, reads in part,

> Every person in parental relation to a minor...Shall furnish proof that a minor who is not attending upon instruction at a public or parochial school...is attending upon required instruction elsewhere. Failure to furnish such proof shall be presumptive evidence that the minor is not attending.

I admit that this rule is not a very onerous one, and it should be a simple matter for a conscientious parent to bring forth evidence that he is in fact providing his child with a reasonable education. Indeed, from the standpoint of judicial convenience it can be argued that a contrary evidentiary rule puts too great a burden on the prosecutor; well, under our system of criminal justice the prosecutor is supposed to be burdened. A more searching objection to such presumptions built into statutes, however, is that they tend very easily to rigidify. In Massachusetts, for example, any persons operating a private school must obtain prior approval from public authorities before it will be assumed that the school provides equivalent education, within the contemplation of an exception clause of the law. If a parent whose child is attending such an unapproved school is charged with violating the compulsory attendance law, he may not, at trial, prove the equivalence of the education imparted by that school. The court won't listen to him. The lack of prior official approval is an irrebuttable presumption, that is, a rule of law, that the education is not equivalent. I submit that such evidentiary rules are ridiculous and a mask for repression.

We have now concluded our survey of the nature, content, and functioning of the compulsory schooling laws. There remains nothing further but to evaluate their efficacy and their future.

Of all the judgments that can be pronounced upon any theory, the most damning is, "it doesn't work." Now it has been contended that parents do have an obligation to educate their children, to prepare them to make their own way in that culture they must someday fully enter. The contrary has been ably argued by scholars I respect. I have not finally concluded in my own mind which side has the better of this debate and, speaking as a lawyer, I really don't care. I don't care because, even when judged within the context of the parental obligation theory that our jurisprudence does in fact assume, on their own terms, the compulsory schooling laws manifestly do not work. They are demonstrably either useless or pernicious, engendering far more compulsion than education.

Some years ago there was a Pennsylvanian named Marsh, who, at the time he makes his first appearance in the law books, had a son, about eight years old. Marsh had some nonconformist ideas concerning health, and refused to have his son vaccinated. He was threatened with criminal prosecution and arrested, not once, but several times since his boy had come of school age, but to no avail. I don't know the outcome of these initial prosecutions, which occurred before Marsh, deciding to counterattack, sued the governor of Pennsylvania in federal court, asking to have him enjoined from enforcing the state's compulsory schooling act, which made vaccination a precondition of school attendance. The court ruled against him, holding that it had no power under the circumstances to restrain any state official, and that Marsh should have exhausted his state remedies, appealing if necessary at last to the United States Supreme Court. While the federal suit was pending, Marsh was convicted again and incarcerated. This time he sued out a writ of habeas corpus against the jail warden and fought it up through the Pennsylvania courts. He lost. At last, several years after Marsh's battles with the compulsory schooling law began, an action was brought *against his son*, seeking to have him declared delinquent and neglected, with a view toward having him removed, if only temporarily, from his father's custody. Even then, the issue was clouded by the delinquency charge, implying some moral fault on the part of the boy. The court, observing that young Marsh had repeatedly presented himself at the school, only to be denied admission, naturally dismissed the delinquency count. But it did hold that the boy was neglected, whereupon he was remanded to the custody of the Pennsylvania Welfare Service, where we may presume he was promptly vaccinated and sent off to school.[24]

Now what is the point of recounting to you this dreary farce bordering on tragedy? Simply this: I defy anyone to tell me how Pennsylvania's compulsory schooling law protected young Marsh's alleged right to an education. During all the years that his father commuted between the courthouse and the jail, what was the law doing to protect the boy? The answer, of course, is absolutely nothing. The law was worse than useless, in that if it had left his father alone at least the son might have gained some degree of education through observation in the home. If the objective of the compulsory schooling laws is to guarantee that children are in fact educated, I fail to see how this goal is furthered by jailing recalcitrant parents. One need not be an expert in the psychopathology of religious fanaticism to understand that penal sanctions, regardless of severity, are ineffective; they beget martyrs, not compliance. Thus, one of the major defects in the compulsory schooling laws is that they are criminal laws.

Both Justice Heffernan of the Wisconsin Supreme Court and Mr. Justice Douglas of the United States Supreme Court wrote dissenting opinions when their respective tribunals passed upon the recent Amish case I mentioned earlier. These dissents were extremely perceptive, and each asked a rather obvious question: What about the rights of the children involved in compulsory schooling disputes? Our American system of law is, for good or ill, an adversary system, and I think it's asking too much of it to expect that antagonists, in the heat of battle, will be scrupulous in their regard for those who, in effect, are third parties under the present law. I have not mentioned the rights of children previously, because the compulsory schooling laws take no account of those rights whatsoever. Setting aside the alleged right to an education, what of the right to due process? During the Wisconsin Amish controversy, the state had the temerity to argue that, even if the law did infringe upon the religious liberty of the Amish parents, the law was in effect directed towards the children, and towards them the state had the right to act in a manner that would be unconstitutional if applied to adults. Such a contention has been rejected by the Supreme Court, which has reaffirmed the principle that children are "persons" to whom the Bill of Rights applies. But mere case-by-case appellate review is not enough. It seems to me that it is incumbent upon the judges of our trial courts, the judges who give to most litigants what is their only day in court, to appoint guardians routinely to protect the rights of children involved in compulsory schooling cases. And just once in a while, it might be a good idea to ask the kids what they think.

Much litigation has arisen out of the question of what constitutes education that is equivalent to that provided in the public schools. In the first place, I submit that this is not a very high standard against which to weigh unconventional modes of teaching youngsters; but in addition, it misses the point. If our theory is that children are entitled to be educated, the test is not to be applied to the means of instruction, but to the child in question. It should be, and in a very few states it is, the uniform rule that, if standardized tests demonstrate that the child is in fact being educated reasonably, then that is the end of the matter, and it is no concern of the law if he's being taught by a guru on a mountain top.

With regard to the health regulations so often tied to compulsory schooling statutes: in the first place, it is absurd and unjust to penalize the child twice—first he is denied a reasonable standard of health care and then as a result he is denied an education as well. If it is granted that parents have an obligation to provide their children with preventive medical treatments, what sense is there in having the penalty for failing in that obligation fall upon the victim? Today, with the almost total eradication of smallpox and diphtheria, I think that the inoculation laws should be abolished. In any event, they should be severed from the education laws.

It is customary today, when discussing education in the United States, to speak in terms of crisis and conflict. We are all aware of the public uproar over busing and other attempts to use the schools for sociological purposes. What is not often noticed is the contribution of compulsory schooling laws to keeping the pot boiling. Busing is not new, of course, but the social goals being promoted today are different from those that were promoted in the past. For example: in 1957, in Virginia, Mr. Dobbins brought his child to school, but the administrators refused to enroll her. She was of the wrong race. Bus transportation was offered to another school, but declined. The impasse was broken when Mr. Dobbins was prosecuted and convicted for violating the compulsory schooling law. In reversing this conviction, the Virginia Supreme Court of Appeals held that Mr. Dobbins had been denied equal protection of the laws, as mandated by the Fourteenth Amendment to the United

States Constitution. Moreover, the court observed, the compulsory education statute may not be applied as a coercive means to require that a citizen give up his constitutional rights.[25] This attitude, it seems to me, marks the direction in which the law is going. In fact, in some places, the courts have gone overboard, to the point of dismissing the rights of children. When some parents removed their children from a New York school that was demonstrably inferior and were charged with child neglect, the court held that

> These parents have the constitutionally guaranteed right to elect no education for their children rather than to subject them to discriminatorily inferior education.[26]

This seems to be going a bit far, since it implies the rejection of the parental obligation theory, but extreme or not, it seems to me to be the judicial trend. This trend is being reinforced by extra-legal social factors tending to expand freedom of choice. While the growth of the so-called counterculture is not yet significant, certainly not numerically, the relatively increased tolerance for varying life styles induced by it in the general population is slowly turning public opinion towards a greater receptivity for innovation in the specific area of education.

Having concluded, rightly or wrongly, that public education is not only failing, but probably beyond redemption, many people, including of course the judges of our courts, are willing to try anything that offers a chance to escape from the present mess; and if this attitude happens to conflict with the compulsory schooling law, well then, so much the worse for the law.

Lest I paint too rosy a picture of the future, let me hasten to assure you that the compulsory schooling laws are *not* going to be abolished. It will take more far-reaching changes than those I have mentioned to bring about a time when the unarticulated political philosophy of the American people will make that possible. Nevertheless, laws can become irrelevant without being repealed. I think that this will happen to the compulsory schooling laws.

NOTES

[1]*Cumming v. Richmond County Board of Education*, 175 U.S. 528 (1899), p. 545.

[2]*Pierce v. Society of Sisters*, 268 U.S. 510 (1925), pp. 534-35.

[3]*Ibid.*, p. 533.

[4]*Stephens v. Bongart*, 15 N.J. Misc. 80 at 92, 189 A. 131 at 137 (Juv. & Dom. Rel. Ct. 1937).

[5]*Ibid.*, at 92, 189 A. at 137.

[6]7 N.J. Super. 608, 72 A. 2d 389 (Cape May County Ct., L. Div. 1950), at 614, 72 A. 2d at 392.

[7]95 N.J. Super. 382, 231 A. 2d 252 (Morris County Ct., L. Div. 1967).

[8]*State v. Garber*, 16 Kan. L. Rev. n. 5 (1968).

[9]404 Ill. 574, 90 N.E. 2d 213 (1950).

[10]*Ibid.*, 215.

[11]55 Wash. 2d 177, 346 P. 2d 999 (1959), cert. denied. 363 U.S. 814(1960).

[12]319 U.S. 624(1943).

[13]*Ibid.*, at 633-34.

[14]370 U.S. 421 (1962). Related case (Bible-reading) is *School Dist. Abington Twp. v. Schempp*, 374 U.S. 203 (1963). Extensive discussion in Leo Pfeffer, *Church, State, and Freedom* rev. ed. (Beacon Press, Boston: undated), pp. 460-78.

[15]Quoted by Black, J., in *Engel v. Vitale*, 370 U.S. 421 (1962).

[16]*Idem.*

[17]*School Bd. v. Thompson*, 24 Okla. 1, 11, 103 P. 578, 582 (1909).

[18]Cited in N.Y. Educ. Law para. 3204 (Historical Note) (McKinney 1970).

[19]*People ex. rel. Vollmar v. Stanley*, 81 Colo. 276, 255 P. 610 (1927), 613, 614.

[20]*Commonwealth v. Bey*, 166 Pa. Super. 136, 70 A. 2d 693 (1950).

[21]*Commonwealth v. Rapine*, 88 Pa. D. & C. 453 (Montgomery County Ct. 1954).

[22]*Commonwealth v. Smoker*, 177 Pa. Super. 435, 110 A. 2d 740 (1955).

[23]49 Wis. 2d 430, 182 N.W.2d 539 (1971), *aff'd*, 40 U.S.L.W. 4476 (May 15, 1972). The *Yoder* decision is founded, at least in part, upon the Wisconsin Supreme Court's interpretation of the First Amendment to the United States Constitution. Thus a federal question is presented. It may well be that the United States Supreme Court wishes to clarify the application of the *Sherbert* rule, particularly in light of the changed membership of the court since *State v. Garber,* 197 Kan. 567, 419 P.2d 896 (1966), *cert. denied,* 389 U.S. 51 (1967). Casad, *supra* note 72, argues cogently that, had the *Garber* court employed the *Sherbert* test, the outcome in that case might have been different. Whatever considerations may underlie the court's decision to review *Yoder,* it is pertinent to note that, had the claim of unconstitutionality advanced in the Wisconsin courts been directed toward the religious liberty provision of the *state* constitution and an analogous ruling obtained, the Amish victory would not have been exposed to jeopardy, since the Supreme Court will not review an interpretation of any state's own constitution made by that state's highest court. *Spector Motor Serv. Inc. v. McLaughlin,* 323

U.S. 101 (1944); *Ashwander v. TVA,* 297 U.S. 288, 345-48 (1936) (Brandeis, J., concurring).

[24]*Marsh v. Earle,* 24 F. Supp. 385 (M.D. Pa. 1938).

[25]*Dobbins v. Commonwealth,* 198 Va. 697, 96 S.E. 2d 154 (1957).

[26]*In re Skipwith,* 14 Misc. 2d 325, 180 N.Y.S. 2d 852 (Dom. Rel. Ct. 1958).

Compulsory education perforce breeds a certain con-formity to the bourgeois values of the school boards and communities. Dr. Joel Henry Spring discovers in state compulsion forces that impair the freedom of minorities, such as the blacks, and which entrench the values and economic status of the privileged classes.

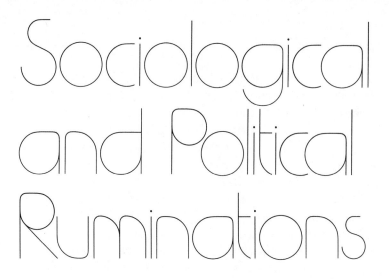

Sociological and Political Ruminations

Joel H. Spring

It is not by accident that mass compulsory schooling has become the midwife of both modern democracy and modern totalitarianism. (Its role is to bring forth the citizen who will support the ideology and structure of the state in word and deed.) Schooling means more than teaching reading and writing or a trade. It means shaping the total character of the individual to meet the political and economic demands of the state. This was the purpose of schooling that wove its way through the dialogue of Plato's *Republic* and found itself stamped into the first major system of mass compulsory schooling (Prussia in the early nineteenth century). It was with this purpose in mind that America's schoolmaster Horace Mann left the arena of law to wage a campaign for the common school. And in the twentieth century both fascism and totalitarian communism found a warm ally in the process of schooling.

Every state develops the process of schooling within the context of belief that it is the possessor of some ideological truth. It is within this framework that schooling is often viewed as the foundation stone of freedom. Freedom, for the modern state, means the right to obey and conform to its laws and ideology. Schooling prepares the individual for freedom by implanting an ideology and fitting individual character to a particular social and political system. David Tyack has shown in a brilliant article[1] that early leaders of the American Republic promoted schooling out of a basic fear that freedom would mean social chaos and mobocracy. The school was viewed as a means of shaping the right character and implanting the right morals for the responsible exercise of freedom—in other words, to produce citizens for the state.

The school as an instrument of the modern state produces the type of citizen who is free to act as his conscience dictates. This assumes that his conscience conforms to the dictates of his schooling. The actual range of action can vary according to the nature of each political system. In one system censorship of written materials can be considered politically justified in terms of maintaining ideological truth. Today in the Soviet Union dissident authors are persecuted for writing poems and novels that are considered destructive of the Soviet way of life. These Soviet writers certainly are not considered as examples of superior products of the system of schooling. On the contrary, they are viewed as failures because their consciences were not correctly molded to the purity of socialist ideals. In the United States, democratic ideology calls for freedom from the pen of the censor, but even here, we are warned that that freedom must be used "responsibly." One is taught not to endanger the morals of a population by allowing a free market in pornography. One is taught that free political journalism can only be maintained if it is used "responsibly." This, of course, means it should not go far enough to rock the ship of state so hard that it capsizes.

What freedom, schooling, and responsibility mean in the United States has been shown by recent public and political reactions to the process of schooling. When students in the 1960s began to act for civil rights and against the war and plutocracy, there was immediate public outcry that the schools were failing to produce good citizens. It was claimed that students were not using their political rights in a responsible manner and it was the job of the school to teach this responsibility. What this meant was that the schools were to teach that democracy meant freedom but not so much freedom that established power was attacked. In state after state in the United States money was withdrawn from the schools. In California a reactionary governor found his way to the capital on a wave of protest against the political actions of students. What has been made quite clear in the last several years is that the schools are the bastions of democratic freedom as long as that freedom does not threaten the position of existing elites.

Schooling must be viewed as a tool by which the state solidifies its power and creates a citizenry. That citizens sometimes rebel is never considered an achievement of mass compulsory schooling but rather its failure. This does not mean schools themselves are conspiracies nor that the teaching of reading and writing is a political plot. Schools, as the term is being used in this essay, mean an institution that consciously attempts to turn men into something. This could be a Communist, a Democrat, a Methodist, or an Amishman. In other words, those who control the schools control a character-producing institution. The real danger of schooling is that it becomes an instrument of power for a ruling elite to maintain and enhance their power over the social system. In a totalitarian system this is precisely the purpose to which the system of schooling directs its attention.

In a democracy schooling endangers the very heart of the political process. Democratic government as it has developed in the United States is based on the idea of the majority electing their representatives, that is, the controllers of the state. One of the virtues of democracy is supposedly the inability of a political and economic elite to gain power and use the state for its own advantage and not the advantage of the majority of the people. In theory the controlling elites in a democracy are accountable to the majority of the population. Elites are displaced as the desires of the electorate change.

The real danger to a democratic process is the establishment of a system of mass, compulsory, and state-regulated schooling. This does not mean that learning, knowledge, and intellectual skills are not beneficial to a democratic system. What is dangerous is a compulsory regulated institution whose purpose is to create something called democratic character. It is through this institution that an elite in a democracy can bend the character of the population to accept the status quo and the power of the ruling institutions, that citizens are led to believe that they should serve their government and not that their government should serve them, that the citizen is led to place the flag above his own conscience and reason, that the poor and the rich learn to accept their respective places in the social system as right and just, that economic leaders can channel the manpower of the nation into selected occupations as if they were dealing with so many pieces of lumber or tons of coal, that man is turned into a thing to be worked upon in the interests of the state.

[That the school can be used in this manner is not accidental.] If one briefly scans the history of arguments in support of schooling, one finds these results were intended. If one briefly looks at present and past schooling in the United States, one can find concrete examples. Take some of the reasons given for support of compulsory schooling in Prussia in the early nineteenth century. One of the more famous and interesting statements was by Johann Gottlieb Fichte in his *Addresses to the German Nation* in 1808.[2] Fichte argued that resistance to the full-scale institution of compulsory schooling would only last for one generation. The first generation affected by compulsory schooling would be schooled into accepting it as a natural part of the process of growing up in Prussia. Fichte also argued that the cost of schooling would be compensated for in terms of the cost of national defense. The schools would produce a citizen who was more willing and able to participate in the army. One could draw many parallels between Fichte's argument in the nineteenth century and the role of schooling in the United States in the twentieth. In the nineteenth century, Prussian teachers were exempted from military service. In the twentieth century the United States government passed a bill with the interesting title of National Defense Education Act. The schools became the front-liners of defense and the teacher was equated with the soldier in serving the needs of the state.

Fichte's important argument was that it won the allegiance and obedience of the citizen to the state. On the one hand this was to be accomplished through the teaching of German history and patriotic exercises. On the other hand, Fichte saw the actual organization of the school and its community of students as the prime producer of citizens for the state. In the twentieth century we would call this the process of *political socialization.* Fichte argued that the child in learning to obey the laws and constitution of the school was being prepared to obey the laws and constitution of the state. The school was a miniature community in which the child learned to adjust his own individuality to the requirements of the community. The real work of the school, Fichte argued, was in shaping this adjustment. The well ordered state required that the citizen go beyond mere obedience to the written constitution and laws. The individual must see the state as something greater than himself and must learn to sacrifice himself for the good of the whole.

Fichte's argument must be considered in terms of recent findings on political socialization and the schools and in terms of democratic ideals. In the United States today the school is the first major public institution encountered in the life of every citizen. It is through one's relationship to the school that one begins to formulate attitudes and modes of action towards other public institutions. *Political socialization studies have found that children learned in elementary school that good citizenship meant obeying the law. In other words, the children rejected an active citizenship for one that was passive and obedient.³ This was a direct result of the very nature of the organization of the elementary school which depended on masses of students obeying the rules of the school and participating in orderly lockstep marches to the playground. Edgar Freidenberg's classic study, *Coming of Age in America*,⁴ found that American high school students viewed the government as a benign institution that one should obey because it was working for the benefit of all people. Freidenberg found that this attitude was fostered by the benign and controlling atmosphere of the school. Students were taught that they had privileges but were without rights. This was fostered within the school by an administration which granted privileges with the attached reminder that if they were not used responsibly they would be withdrawn. Students were socialized to accept that in the United States people did not have irrevocable civil rights but had privileges granted through the good will of a benign government. Their attitudes were like a woman I once heard who suggested that all people should be fingerprinted by the government. After all, she stated, if you are good and obey the law, it won't matter.

Fichte's arguments favoring the political socialization of mass schooling received added support and elaboration in the United States. In this country the argument was interwoven with the somewhat contradictory idea that a democracy could only survive if there was an institution that produced democratic men and a democratic culture with a consensus of values and beliefs. The great spokesman for the common school, Horace Mann, argued that a republican government required the sharing of a common set of republican values and moral principles. The common school, by bringing the rich and the poor together, would melt away the animosity between social classes. The rich and the poor together within the four walls of the classroom would be taught the common republican principles on which our political system rested. From the great Christian tradition would be taught those moral principles with which all religions could agree. The common school was to produce the common man with the common culture and ideology. Social, economic, and political strife was to be eliminated through the institution of common schooling.[5]

To a certain extent Mann's dream of the common school has been fulfilled. With a slow, crushing grind the school has attempted to obliterate the cultural differences existing within the United States. Catholics have attempted to keep their heads above water by maintaining their own schools. The Amish have recently won a reprieve in their battle against compulsory schooling. But with many Americans the school has achieved its objective.

Mann envisioned the school as not only creating the democratic consensus but also preventing social transgressions. The school would become the enforcer of the law. It would be the experiment in government that would succeed beyond the scope of previous social organizations. Within the school the law and morality of society would be internalized so that criminal transgression throughout the land would be eliminated. Men would no longer commit criminal acts or lead immoral lives because within the schoolroom they would learn to be righteous. The law of the land and society would be internalized in every citizen through the mechanism of the schoolmaster and the schoolhouse.[6]

Now the important question that must be asked of both the political socialization of Fichte and the common school idea of Horace Mann is *whose* political society, *whose* political and moral consensus, and *whose* social laws will the school reflect? In other words, after the machinery of political and social control is established, who will give substance to the ideals? In the United States the source of interpretation and direction is the local boards of education. But who controls these local boards? From the beginning of the century to the present, studies of the social composition of school boards show that they are dominated by upper-class business and professional people.[7] This is truer in small town and urban areas than in farm areas. In urban areas it is not accidental. Urban school reform at the beginning of the century was consciously directed towards eliminating local ward control in favor of centralized school boards.[8] It was believed reasonable and beneficial to the process of schooling to assure its domination by elites.

The social composition of school boards in the United States has assured that the political and social ideals of the public schools would reflect conservative and reactionary ideals. The schools are made the market place for the Chamber of Commerce, American Legion, Daughters of the American Revolution, Rotary Clubs, Kiwanis Clubs, and other such organizations to peddle their wares. Before World War II it was even difficult to get conservative labor union material into the school. Because of this type of control the schools have naturally become havens for Bank Day, Junior Achievement, ROTC, Junior Kiwanis Clubs, and Chamber of Commerce celebrations.

Now it should be reiterated that the problem is not one of refining the methods of control of compulsory, state-regulated schooling. It is inevitable that compulsory, state-regulated schooling will reflect the political philosophy of the status quo. It is after all those who

have political and social power who gain the most benefit from the existing political climate and depend on its
continuation. It seems illogical to think of a group with a
particular political philosophy supporting a system of
schooling that instilled its opposite. It is inevitable that
the process of political socialization and the development
of a political and moral consensus should reflect the organization of the existing state and those who control
that state.

It is also inevitable that when the school attempts to
serve the economic ends of the state it reinforces and
perpetuates the existing class structure. Following the
political and social arguments of Fichte and Mann came
the economic arguments for mass schooling. By the end
of the nineteenth century it was felt that schools were
needed for the production of workers to meet the needs
of the developing corporate state. Workers had to be
trained and sorted for their particular places in the industrial system. The educational methods developed for
this social selection included intelligence tests, vocational
guidance, differentiation of courses of study, ability
grouping, and the comprehensive high school. In the
twentieth century it was the comprehensive high school
that would be the great creator of the democratic consensus and the social sorting machine for the corporate
state. Trapped in the rhetoric of meeting individual differences, the school would use intelligence tests to separate students according to abilities. Achievement tests,
interest tests, and career counseling would be used to
help the student choose a future vocation and related
educational track in the school.[9]

What has been the result of this social sorting? Study
after study has shown this process of differentiation resulting in the school reflecting the class structure of the

surrounding society. When students are separated according to ability by either teachers or intelligence tests, the upper ability groups are inevitably populated by children from upper social and economic groups, and the lower ability groups by children from lower social and economic classes. The same results are found when tracking systems are investigated. Those in the college preparatory tracks are primarily from upper social and economic groups and those in the vocational track are from lower social and economic classes.[10]

As the school reflects the social class structure of the surrounding community, it also reinforces that class structure. Students are schooled into their social place. The school becomes the first arena of social competition. It is the first indicator of the winners in the social race. Except for the few who slip through to the higher areas of the school structure, most of the poor are taught by the process of school differentiation that they should accept their station in life. Except for the few who slip to the bottom of the school structure, most of the children of affluence learn that it is right and just that they should be at the top of the social pile.

No amount of psychological gimmickry will change this situation. The search for the golden egg of a culturally free indicator of native intelligence is a hopeless quest. What is defined and prized as intelligence is dependent on the nature of the existing society and the type of individual characteristics required to succeed within that type of society. These behavioral characteristics are generated within the environment that surrounds the child during his early years. Inherited abilities are shaped and given direction by these forces. To create equal conditions for upbringing might require forms of communal child-rearing such as the Israeli kibbutz. But day care centers and communal child-rearing proposals take one back to the problem of who will determine the behavioral characteristics that will be nurtured within these communal environments. Day care centers and communal child-rearing might contribute greatly to the cause of female emancipation, but their value in creating an equal social race is tempered by their openness to abuse by becoming instruments of political and economic control.

One example of all these various shades of control and the power of the school is the history of schooling in the southern states of the United States. Here is a clear example of the use of the school as a means of economic power and as a means of maintaining a particular form of social stratification. The development of a segregated system of schooling in the South in the late nineteenth century was not accidental but was the result of conscious plans by industrial leaders to segregate the black population and educate them as an inexpensive labor force for the new industrial South. Henry Allen Bullock's fine *History of Negro Education in the South* carefully documents industrial involvement in the creation and development of segregated schools. The work of historian James Anderson shows the prominent role industrial leaders played in developing Booker T. Washington's ideas on the industrial education of the black man and spreading those ideas throughout the South.[11]

Segregated mass schooling maintained and assured the continuation of a segregated society in the South. The school institutionalized a whole process of cultural segregation and assured that it would play a major part in shaping the character of blacks and whites. The Supreme Court decision that ended segregated schooling was based on a recognition of the extreme social power of the school. What was overlooked was that integration of the schools would not necessarily close the gap. Southern schools have armed themselves with the weapons used by schools in the North. Segregation can be carried out within the school with the refined weapons of grouping, meeting individual differences, intelligence tests, tracking, special education, classes for "behavior problems" and other forms of differentiation. The desegregation of the schools will not destroy the power of the school to continue its segregation.

 Now the problems of political control, consensus ideology, and social stratification are not just leaks in the roof of the American schoolhouse. The problem is with the very foundation of the structure. We must build a new foundation and structure which will assure that no particular social or political ideology can dominate and control the socialization process of a whole society of children. We need an educational system that will assure that schools cannot serve as the bulwarks of the status quo and reinforce social and economic inequalities; a system men can use, not a system that uses men; a system that does not have the purpose of producing citizens who exist for the maintenance of the state.

A system of education should also be built on a foundation that does not pretend that schooling will eliminate or cure the problems of crime, poverty, or social injustice. To say that schooling will solve these problems is to say that the structure of society is sound and that it is the individual who must change to fit that society. To use schooling to solve these problems is to maintain the status quo by avoiding the examination and change of the social structure that caused these problems. To tell the poor that poverty will end with their completion of schooling is to place the blame for their poverty on their shoulders and not on the structure of society. All the process of schooling accomplishes is to condemn the majority of poor who lose in the schooling race and teach them that society is correct and they are the problems.

A new system of education should no longer function as a midwife to the state and to its concept of the citizen. The changes must be basic. Educational discussions that center around things like open classroom, pass-fail, schools without failure, and other gimmicks, are talking only about band-aid treatments. Changes must be made at the basic levels of funding, educational requirements, certification, and the family.

Now I would like to mention some areas where change is needed. One area is the concept of certification. Issuance of diplomas and degrees is one of the most important means by which mass schooling maintains its social power. With the complete triumph of compulsory schooling in the twentieth century the school as a social sorting machine has become the central certification system for entrance into different occupational levels. High school and college diplomas became standard requirements on job applications. In many cases, the diplomas, as has been pointed out many times, have little direct connection to the actual requirements in many occupational areas. What is the difference between a person who does not take a required English course or physical education course and consequently fails to receive a high school diploma, and one who does take the course and receives the diploma? Why should the one with the degree be considered a superior candidate for a job as mail clerk or stock boy? The diploma madness has infected students and schools with a constant concern for getting the correct number of credits in the required areas of schooling. Diplomas turn schooling into working for grades in required courses to achieve a piece of paper for entrance into the job market.

Eliminating the traditional concept of the diploma and its control of certification would be an important step in changing the nature of schooling. Internally it would create immediate changes. Grades would lose meaning and required courses would disappear. One would take a course of study in order to learn something. Learning would no longer be attached to running the race for a diploma. No longer would people think in terms of organizing a curriculum to produce able citizens. Also changes in attitudes and organization would result if one went to something called a high school or college and there was no diploma to be earned. The power to demand certain outcomes from learning would be removed and with it part of the political and social power of the school.

The elimination of the diploma system would lead to a whole reconsideration of the process of certification. Certainly there are areas where it is important that there exist public recognition of knowledge; for example, medicine. One certainly needs to know that a surgeon knows surgery before he operates on you. With this situation one could still have professional schools designed to produce certain types such as doctors, lawyers, and engineers. But even here a diploma does not guarantee competence. In the case of medicine there must be some community involvement in the certification process and public knowledge of actual ability. For instance, one could even consider the publication of a local medical kill rate. The whole area of alternative methods of certification for professions is one of the important things that must be considered in terms of the future of our social system.

Coupled with the elimination of the traditional diploma must be the limitation of most state control of education. This would mean the elimination of compulsory schooling and the limitation of governmental educational requirements. The objective of this goal would be to decrease the possibility of education being used by an elite group to form a particular political and social character and to reinforce an existing social class structure. To achieve this end it is desirable to minimize government requirements and control over educational institutions. In the United States, schools have attained a bland sameness because of curriculum requirements and requirements for certification of teachers. Probably the worst thing that ever happened to education was governmental control of teacher certification. Not only have certification requirements populated the school staffs with intellectual mediocrity but they have also contributed to the controlling elements of a consensus ideology and culture in the United States. Schools and government school bureaus have tended to operate on the principle espoused by Horace Mann in the nineteenth century—that we can tolerate some eccentricities in our neighbors but we cannot tolerate them in our teachers who are to be social mirrors for all children.

What might be considered and should be discussed as national educational requirements are levels of competence in reading, writing, and arithmetic. This would minimize the government's involvement in education to the level of teaching skills and not producing citizens. Thomas Jefferson believed that the mass requirements for schooling could be limited to three years. During this period the future citizens of the Republic were taught how to read and write. Jefferson trusted the reason and the common sense of the people to develop their own opinions within the arena of a free press. He did not consider using the schools to shape all men into democrats but to provide the tools by which men could democratize themselves. Any discussion of educational requirements must consider the difference between schooling that moulds men into something, and education that men acquire for their own private purposes.

The issue of compulsory schooling must be approached from several directions. In the first place, the concept of compulsory schooling as an instrument by which the state assures itself of a loyal citizenry is repugnant and harmful to the democratic process. It is in this area that Americans must rethink the relationship between the individual and the state. Men should not exist to be trained and shaped to serve the state but should have the state serving them. In the second place, the concept of compulsory education as a cure for the economic displacement caused by technology must be reconsidered. One reason for compulsory education was the shift from a rural, agricultural economy to an urban industrial state. With this shift arose arguments that the exploitation of children could only be overcome by the establishment of child labor laws and forced attendance at school. It was also argued that urban children, as compared to rural children who played important roles around the farm, were socially and economically without a meaningful function in the city. Increased juvenile delinquency at the turn of the century was often linked to the idea that children and youth in the modern urban and industrial world got into trouble because of boredom and a lack of activities. Compulsory schooling was to create a holding institution that kept children and youth occupied and off the labor market.

The argument for the expansion of schooling as a solution for technological displacement has been increasingly used in the twentieth century. As productivity has increased, a lower percentage of the population has been required in the work force. In other words, in the United States in the twentieth century there has been an actual decrease in the percentage of the population involved in production. This, of course, is one of the promises of technology. More leisure is supposedly the goal of our industrial civilization. The first group that this affected was youth. During the 1920s high school became a mass institution that assured a whole age group's removal from the labor market, and after World War II the general extension of schooling through the college years increased the percentage of the population removed from the labor force. Also after World War II there was a general increase in retirement for people over 65, further reducing the percentage of population involved in production. It is interesting that this development has led to the expansion of schooling and demands for increased schooling for the retired.[12] In the nineteenth century, schooling was supported because of a fear of the masses' experiencing freedom and in the twentieth century because of a fear of the masses' experiencing leisure.

Compulsory schooling as a means of institutionalizing non-productive segments of the population is not a creative solution to one of the major problems resulting from increased technology. In fact, it avoids direct confrontation with the problem of an increasingly dehumanized society with man becoming a mere consuming appendage to technology. The elimination of compulsory schooling must take place in an environment that is willing to see the nature of modern technology as one of the important issues that must be discussed. The school now fills a void of empty time created by modern industrialism. Before technology continues on its present path, we must begin to discuss the possibility of creating a technology that men can use as a means of self-expression in creating their own worlds. We need a technological society in which all men have an integrated and creative role.

The elimination of compulsory mass schooling must also be considered in terms of the nature of the family and role of women in society. Schooling in the nineteenth century always contained an internal contradiction with regard to women and the family. On the one hand, the school prepared women to assume a direct role in the commercial and business world of society. On the other hand, the school depended on the basic family of husband as bread-winner and woman as housewife. The economic support of children flows through this basic institution of the family. It should be recognized that the school has not weakened the family but has strengthened it. In fact, increased schooling in the twentieth century has lengthened the number of years that children are economically dependent on the family structure. Women have felt the frustration of their school training coming into conflict with the demand for maintenance of the family. Equality for women will not take place until this family structure is changed.

The elimination of compulsory schooling and the integration of children and youth into a creative technological society would make possible the liberation of women from this structure of family. It would also make possible the elimination of marriage. This would require a reconsideration of the problem of financial support of education and children. One possibility is a voucher system where at birth all children are granted some set sum. The danger of some of the present voucher proposals is that they reinforce the existing family structure by giving that unit the responsibility for use of the voucher. One way of avoiding this might be to give control of the voucher directly to the child with some brief period of parental control.

The effect of the elimination of compulsory mass schooling on the family highlights the meaning of the school as a central institution of modern society. Any basic changes in the foundation of the school will affect all aspects of our society. In fact, while we may discuss the issues, there may be little we can do, because the problem is broad and interrelated with all aspects of society. The situation is similar to that of a medical doctor who recognized that his patient has an incurable case of cancer. He can study and talk about the cancer but he cannot cure it. At this point we can study mass compulsory schooling as a primary instrument of political and social control and recognize its power in segregating and strengthening social classes; but, because the school is so intimately related to all social problems, any cure requires a total transformation of society. Changing the modern state, technology, and the family is a very broad and sweeping order. But discussion of these issues is not academic, just as it is not academic for the medical doctor to discuss the problems of and possible cures for cancer.

NOTES

[1]David Tyack, "Forming the National Character: Paradox in the Educational Thought of the Revolutionary Generation," *Harvard Educational Review*, Vol. 36, No. 1 (Winter, 1966), pp. 29-41.

[2]Johann Fichte, *Addresses to the German Nation*, trans. by R. F. Jones (Chicago, Open Court Publishing, 1922), pp. 19-52.

[3]"Political Socialization," *Harvard Educational Review*, Vol. 38, No. 3 (Summer, 1968).

[4]Edgar Friedenberg, *Coming of Age in America* (New York: Vintage, 1963).

[5]Horace Mann, *Massachusetts Board of Education, Twelfth Annual Report* (1848).

[6]*Ibid.*

[7]George Sylvester Counts, *The Social Composition of Boards of Education* (Chicago: University of Chicago Press, 1927); Roy M. Caughran, "The School Board Member Today," *American School Board Journal* (November, 1956); *Report of the National Boards Association*, 1965.

[8]Joel H. Spring, *Education and the Rise of the Corporate State* (Boston: Beacon, 1972), Ch. IV.

[9]*Ibid.*

[10]See Patricia Cayo Sexton, *Education and Income* (New York: Viking Press, 1961), and Robert E. Herriott and Nancy Hoyt St. John, *Social Class and the Urban School* (New York: John Wiley, 1966).

[11]Henry Allen Bullock, *A History of Negro Education in the South* (New York: Praeger, 1967).

[12]Joel H. Spring, "Development of Youth Culture in the United States," published in *The Roots of Crisis: American Education in the Twentieth Century* (Chicago: Rand McNally, 1972).

There are strong indications that people would over-whelmingly seek the education they and their children need—because of its utility—without truancy laws and school taxes. Professor E. G. West explores these economic factors, and describes what happened in the 19th century when fee-charging schools gave way to tax-supported ones. (Some of Professor West's technical analysis has not been included in this edition.)

Economic Analysis Positive and Normative

E. G. West

The full complexity of the economic consequences of conventional types of compulsion cannot be grasped without some knowledge of historical circumstances. In the era of the nineteenth century social reform there was genuine and growing concern for children who were deprived in all senses—not just in the area of education. All kinds of public policies were devised to discriminate in favor of these children, including measures to protect them from malnutrition, parental cruelty, poor housing, and inadequate clothing. Laws were so operated as to discipline irresponsible parents selectively. Since it was rarely suggested that the delinquent families were in the majority, these *discriminatory* measures were usually considered sufficient. Those parents who were coerced by the law to treat their children better—as in food and raiment—were in effect subject to compulsion but it was *selective* compulsion.

The case of education developed differently; here *universal* compulsion was applied. At first sight there seems no difference. Universally applicable laws, it will be argued, should not affect responsible families, since they will already be doing what the law wants them to do. Deeper investigation shows there was an important difference. In Britain just before universal compulsion (in the 1860s) there was a near-universal system of private fee-paying schools, and the majority of parents were using it. In 1870 it was thought necessary to *complement* this system with a few government schools ("board schools") in those areas where there was proved insufficiency. In 1880, universal compulsion was legislated. It was next argued that since the government could not force parents to do something they could not afford, schooling should be made "free." Free schooling should be available even to the majority of parents who were previously paying for it as well as to the minority that the legislation was ostensibly aimed at. Free schooling required full subsidization. It was next argued that only the new government ("board") schools could fully qualify for such treatment. Private schools that were run for a profit should not be aided because this practice would subsidize profit-makers. (This anti-profit principle was incorporated into every piece of nineteenth-century legislation). Most of the remaining private schools were connected with the churches. It was argued that it would be wrong to treat these as favorably as the "board schools" because that would be using Catholic taxpayers' contributions to subsidize Protestant schools and vice-versa. The result was that the new "board schools" originally set up to *complement* a private system eventually *superseded* it. Many, if not most, of those who originally advocated compulsion were supporters of voluntary church schools. In the particular way in which compulsion was enacted (*universal* as distinct from *selective* compulsion) there were significant effects upon the majority of parents who did not need it. For them it became in effect *compulsion to change from one school system to another.* Since this new (collectivized) system was associated with a growing educationist bureaucracy and a protection-seeking teaching profession that was among the strongest of nineteenth-century agitators for universal compulsion, it is possible that universal compulsion eventually led to *less* total schooling in real terms, or in terms related to family preference, than would otherwise have resulted (bear in mind that education is a normal good, the supply of which would have increased "voluntarily" following the increases in income and population that actually occurred after 1880).

The argument that where schooling was made compulsory the government had an obligation to see to it that poor parents could pay the necessary fees goes back as far as the Report on the Handloom Weavers in 1841, which was largely written by Nassau Senior. It appears on page 123: "It is equally obvious that if the State be bound to require the parent to educate his child, it is bound to see that he has the means to do so." [1] In his *Principles* published seven years later, John Stuart Mill similarly argued:

It is therefore an allowable exercise of the powers of gov-

ernment to impose on parents the legal obligation of giving elementary instruction to children. This, however,
cannot fairly be done, without taking measures to insure
that such instruction shall always be accessible to them either gratuitously or at a trifling expense.[2]

Mill's basic case for the establishment of compulsion
rested on his belief that the voluntary principle had
failed to supply sufficient instruction.

> . . . I shall merely express my conviction that even in
> quantity it is (in 1848) and is likely to remain altogether
> insufficient. . .[3]

Notice that this was not an appeal to systematic evidence. National data were not available until the 1851
Census Report on Education in England and Wales.
This revealed in fact over two million day scholars. Mill
was arguing from impressionism, from a "conviction."
He had a very firm opinion that "the uncultivated cannot be competent judges of cultivation." The voluntary
principle failed because ". . . the end not being desired,
the means will not be provided at all. . ."[4]

If Mill and his supporters had been more willing to
have their views efficiently tested by the evidence, they
might not have been so hasty in recommending *universal* compulsion. Careful reflection would have shown
that it was difficult to distinguish between parental
"negligence" and parental indigence. Countless observers in the nineteenth century condemned parents for
their *irresponsibility*, and then, after compulsion was established, urged that the fees should be abolished to en-
able them to overcome their *poverty*. The only sure way
to disentangle these issues is to subsidize the fees first;
only then, after a suitable time lag, will the real preferences of parents reveal themselves. Furthermore, one
should add to the total amount available for subsidy the

funds that would otherwise be spent on policing a compulsory system.

Hitherto historians of education have been unanimous that the evidence shows that compulsion did significantly increase attendance in the twenty or thirty years after the legislation. Their argument is inadequate for four reasons. The first relates to the point just made. Among the other things that happened in addition to compulsion was the steady reduction of fees. This reduction works in the direction of expanding the demand for schooling (provided that the subsidies do not come entirely from extra taxes on the beneficiaries). Second, the per capita national income was increasing during those years. This means that, provided education was a normal good (with a positive income elasticity of demand)[5] the voluntary demand for it even as a consumption good would have increased anyway. It is true that the opportunity costs of schooling (forgone earnings) would have increased and this would have worked in the opposite direction. Still other forces were pushing in favor of expansion, however. There was, for instance, a secular decline in loan interest, a circumstance that tends to increase the incentive to invest in more schooling. Again the secular fall in the death rate must have had a similar influence.

Third, there was a steady expansion of population. Growth of voluntary attendance in absolute terms would have occurred for this reason alone. (Several historians do acknowledge this point). Fourth, many observers have quoted figures of increased enrollment following compulsion at *public* ("board") schools. Much of this increase, however, was the result of a switching from private schools. The switching occurred because the public schools were increasingly forcing others out of the market by subsidized fees.

In their regression analysis of nineteenth-century compulsory legislation in the U.S., Landes and Solmon found (1972) that in 1880 the average level of schooling was greater in states with compulsory laws than in states without them when other independent variables, such as state income, the number of foreign immigrants, population density, etc., were held constant. But they emphasized that it was not possible to conclude from this that compulsory legislation was the *cause* of higher levels of schooling. The possibility remained that differences in schooling between states with and without compulsory laws pre-dated these laws. Further investigation revealed that this in fact was the case. They concluded that school legislation was definitely not the cause of higher schooling levels:

> Instead these laws appear to have merely formalized what was already an observed fact; namely, that the vast majority of school age persons had already been obtaining a level of schooling equal to or greater than what was to be later specified by statute.[6]

In Britain the nineteenth-century data are less accessible and more fragmented. Compulsion was initiated by thousands of local school boards when they were set up after 1870. One has the strong immediate impression that in the short run there was some significant influence. But there were different circumstances in Britain and the U.S. In many parts of America universal free schooling was established before compulsion. For instance in New York State the Free Schools Act finally abolished fees (parental rate bills) in 1867. The New York Education Act establishing compulsion was passed seven years later. In Britain compulsion came first and the trend towards heavily subsidized fees and eventually zero prices came *after*. The causal connection between compulsion and enrollment is therefore more difficult to elicit in the British case, because the move towards free schooling could have been a strong influence in expanding enrollments. A stronger *apparent* effect of the compulsory legislation in Britain might therefore be explained in these terms.

Our analysis so far has assumed that compulsion is fully enforced. In practice enforcement is a variable; its success is proportional to the resources devoted to it. After the nineteenth-century legislation, truancy did not cease completely; and it has not done so to this day. Indeed in New York, it was reported in 1970 that the Board of Education "can no longer enforce" the state's compulsory schooling law "because of the high rate of truancy."[7] Minimum school laws impose an expected penalty depending on the probability of being caught and the probability of legal proceedings. This cost will vary in subjective terms depending on personal disutility from non-compliance and on risk aversion. If "too much" compulsion is enforced there is the danger of large scale parental "rebellion," and the law is brought into disrepute.

In a paper read before the British Association in the 1970s a Professor Jack questioned the wisdom of the authorities in Birmingham in being so proud of their above-average attendance increases. These were obtained, he said, with especially stringent enforcement measures. Whereas the average attendance increase in Glasgow, after compulsion was adopted in that city, was 25 per cent per annum, with prosecutions of one in 20,000 of the population, the average increase in Birmingham was 31 per cent and the prosecutions one in 200.

Joseph Chamberlain retorted that Birmingham was *not* being tougher than Glasgow. In Scotland, although there were fewer convictions, the penalities were more severe. The actual amount of the Glasgow penalty was in many cases 40 shillings, whereas the maximum penalty in England was five shillings. The fear of the heavier Scotch penalty was an even bigger deterrent.

More interesting in Chamberlain's reply is his argument that the biggest cause of increased attendance in Birmingham was the drastic reduction in school fees. The Birmingham school board was exceptional in these reductions. It had lowered fees in many cases to one penny whereas the typical board school fee was three pennies. Chamberlain discovered (in economist's jargon) an elasticity of demand for education that was greater than unity:

> As regards the boys' and girls' schools in which the penny fee has been adopted, the result has been very remarkable, and to some of us, at all events, very satisfactory. Wherever the fees have been reduced, the total amount of fees received in a given period after the reduction has exceeded the total amount of fees received....in other words, the reduction of fees in every case has trebled the attendance....I can only say that my experience since I have sat upon this board confirms me in the opinion that if we could have universal free schools in England, as they exist in America, France, Sweden, Norway, Denmark and many other countries, we should reduce the necessity of compulsion to a minimum, even if we did not do away with it altogether.[8]

The findings of Landes and Solmon that school legislation in the U.S. did not cause higher schooling levels in the nineteenth century leave us with an obvious problem. Why was such an elaborate administration for universal compulsion set up if its achievements were so small? The modern branch of positive economics known as "the economics of politics" may give some insight. It will be helpful to consider first another example of "individual failure": inadequate feeding or individual malnutrition.[9] Suppose that two people out of a community of one thousand cannot be trusted to feed themselves or their children adequately and that such irresponsibility is regarded as a social detriment. What is the most viable policy for a politician whose behavior is attuned to vote maximization? If a *universal* degree of compulsion is to be established, this could involve substantial policing costs including the costs of inspecting and checking not only the eating habits of the two delinquents but also those of the remaining 998. Compare this situation with one wherein, say, about 450 out of the 1,000 are likely to be delinquents. At first sight it may appear that the case for *universal* (as distinct from selective) compulsion is less substantial in the first situation with two "delinquents" than in the second with 450. When political considerations enter, however, the position appears more complex. Making nearly half of the electorate do something they have no wish to do is clearly a policy that stands to lose more votes than one that coerces only two people.

The result seems paradoxical. Other things being equal, compulsion is more "profitable" to the government the smaller the minority to be compelled. Yet the needs of the children of a small minority of "irresponsible" parents may be met more efficiently if the paternalistic powers of government were concentrated on them, and not diffused over wide areas where they are not needed. Ideally, compulsion should be selective and not universal. Where *universal* compulsion is too readily applied, the authorities may shelter themselves too com-

fortably from pressures to improve facilities. Where
there is no compulsion to stay on at school in the six-
teenth or seventeenth year, the suppliers of formal
"education" (the schools) are in competition with informal but efficient alternative forms of education such as
apprenticeships and learning on the job. The obligation
constantly to "lure" young people into additional schooling puts constant pressure upon schools and teachers to
be imaginative and efficient. Conversely, the protection-
ist instinct of schools leads them into alliance with governments to support compulsion. This hypothesis was
previously put forward in an article in 1967,[10] where it
was concluded that in the U.S. context:

> Especially since public money was distributed to the
> schools and their staffs in proportion to the numbers in
> attendance, we should expect that the kind of agitation
> that would next have been undertaken (after fees had
> been successfully abolished) by the income maximizing
> teachers, managers and the officials, especially those of av-
> erage or less than average ability, would have been a cam-
> paign for an education that was compulsory by statute.[11]

The historical evidence in America supported the hypothesis:

> Serious agitation for compulsory attendance by bureau
> officials and teachers built up very soon after the success
> of the free school campaign of 1867.[12]

Landes and Solmon now conclude that their findings are
also consistent with this sort of explanation:

> On the demand side, two forces would be at work to in-
> crease the demand for compulsory legislation. First teach-
> ers and school officials are likely to favor and promote
> legislation that compels persons to purchase their prod-
> uct; namely schooling. As enrollment and attendance
> rates rise and the length of the school year increases, the
> number of teachers and school officials also increases.

Along with a growth in their number, we expect an increase in their power to influence legislators to support a compulsory law. On the supply side...with a growth of schooling levels, the number of parents opposed to the enactment of the law would obviously decline.[13]

There is similar evidence in English history. Almost without exception the nineteenth century government inspectors wanted compulsion.[14] Matthew Arnold, school inspector for the Metropolitan District of Westminster, seems at first sight to have been an exception. In 1867 he thought compulsion was not appropriate to England. "In Prussia, which is so often quoted, education is not flourishing because it is compulsory, it is compulsory because it is flourishing.... When instruction is valued in this country as it is in Germany it may be made obligatory here...."[15] This objection obviously related only to the question of timing; compulsion should be established when everybody, or nearly everybody, prized culture so much that voluntary instruction would be universal. The question why the "means" of universal compulsion should be applied after the "ends" had already largely been obtained was not raised by Arnold. It was in the interests of his fellow inspectors and his department that it was not. But despite his doubts about direct compulsion Arnold was a strong advocate of *indirect* compulsion. This, in 1867, was the better expedient:

> The persevering extension of provisions for the schooling of all children employed in any kind of labour is probably the best and most practicable way of making education obligatory that we can at present take.[16]

Along with the Inspectorate and the Education Department, the proprietors of schools also advocated compulsion. While the voluntary school managers objected to the setting up of board *schools* that were able to compete unfairly, they were not opposed to the setting up of school *boards* where this was done (as the act allowed) to organize compulsion and finance to help the poor pay the voluntary school fees. Mr. Bowstead in his report testified to this attitude:

> It by no means follows that, if once such a supply of voluntary schools were secured, the same objections would continue to be raised to the establishment of school boards. On the contrary there is among school managers, both lay and clerical, a very strong desire to be armed with the powers conferred upon school boards by the recent statute.[17]

If compulsion does cause (or prolong) lethargy among monopoly suppliers of schooling, the reform will be perverse. This point was grasped a century ago in America. When, in 1871, the school suppliers of education in New York State were lamenting their loss of income because of "early leaving," the superintendent remonstrated:

> It is palpable that the prominent defect, that calls for speedy reformation, is not incomplete attendance, but poor teaching....I speak of the needed improvement in the particular mentioned, in comparison with compulsion, as a means of securing attendance; and I contend, that, before sending out ministers of the law to force children to school, we should place genuine teachers in the school room to attract them...the improvement in question should be made before resorting to the doubtful experiment of compulsion. It cannot be done suddenly by legislation.[18]

The superintendent's proposal however was defeated. The influence of the teachers' political lobby was already too strong for him.

It is consistent with the hypothesis of political "profit

(vote) maximizing" that politicians under pressure from, or in alliance with, the factor supply interest groups, will have an incentive to make the electorate believe that the problem of delinquency is greater than it really is. One way of fostering this illusion is to make each parent think that, in confidence, compulsion is not intended for *his* particular children; for this would indeed be a reflection on the parent in question and the politician does not want to alienate him. The politician will be on better ground if he suggests that compulsion is perhaps really needed for some of his (unspecified) neighbors who are less obviously reliable. Indeed it is possible that in such a way the more compulsion that is established the more the "good" individual families may believe that "bad" families exist. By such a process, the status of the politician grows in proportion as that of "the average parent" deteriorates.

The supposed "need" to raise the compulsory leaving age in Britain affords an interesting example. For an objective observer the key information is the precise number of *actual* "delinquents" who would fail to stay on voluntarily. Conventional questionnaires often yield information on this that is too superficial. The measure of the parental demand for education should relate to *efficient* education. A measure that expresses the willingness to stick with inefficient surroundings is a quite different and inadequate one. All British observers, including the politicians, have admitted in the last ten years that schools have been overstretched, buildings substandard, and teachers too few. The true numbers "who wish to stay on" cannot adequately be assessed until they have been given effective opportunities, and time, to decline the offer of efficient and available facilities. As the Crowther Report put it in 1959:

> ...good educational facilities, once provided, are not left
> unused; they discover or create a demand that public
> opinion in the past has been slow to believe exist-
> ed....many boys and girls are at present deprived of ed-
> ucational facilities which they would use well and which
> they are legally entitled to receive.[19]

Since 1959 the demand for schooling has been increasing in proportion to the supply of facilities. In
these circumstances it is certainly not easy to say to what
extent "compulsion" is a necessary additional stimulus to
the provision of good facilities. We cannot know with
any accuracy until those facilities *are* provided. Meanwhile, emphasis upon compulsion may be "politically expedient," but to the citizen it may well be dangerous in
that it may involve a wrong definition of the problem.

So far we have employed positive economics; this pro-
ceeds by prediction and the testing of hypotheses with
the facts. Normative economics, to which we now turn, is
concerned with what "ought to be" rather than with
what is. Traditional normative analysis has been rooted
in the welfare economics of Pareto, which assumes that
each individual is to count and that each is the best
judge of his own interest. A Pareto optimum *point* is
one where any change will harm at least one person in
society. A Pareto optimum *move* is one that benefits at
least one person and harms nobody.

In one sense if we take the family to be the basic unit,
and if the new laws are to "bite," the establishment of
compulsion will not pass the Pareto criteria because it
will injure some individuals; it will not be a Pareto *move*.
It is possible, however, to achieve a given level of schooling without injury if simultaneous compensation is paid.
If compulsion is accompanied by the introduction of
"free" education, the financial benefit of the reduced ed-

ucation costs to the family may provide this compensation. The family could rationally vote for such a move (although there is still considerable fiscal illusion concerning which taxpayers pay for what). The direct expenses of schooling (the fees) are not the only costs, however. In some cases, indirect costs, notably in the shape of the loss of foregone earnings, will be critical. While the social benefits are positive, the private benefits may be negative. With reference to low achievers, W. Hansen, B. A. Weisbrod, and W. Scanlon have concluded, "They are unlikely to benefit financially unless an attempt is made to insure that they offer valuable opportunities, such as training programs, to enhance their earning power."[20] In all these cases it will be necessary to compensate the family not only with schooling subsidies (or vouchers) but also with income replenishments.[21] It should be emphasized that where compulsion *is* accompanied by appropriate compensation it no longer has the implications of strong coercion. Where income supplements are given to encourage schooling, the function of compulsion is similar to the "compulsion" implied in any contract to deliver goods or to provide specific services.

If there is a genuine redistribution, that is if the beneficiaries are receiving "subsidies" that are not financed through taxes upon themselves, normative welfare economics must explore the possible motives of those in society who voluntarily vote to have funds transferred away from them for the schooling of others. One common explanation is that the consumption of schooling by one person in Group A enters measurably into the utility of those persons making up Group B. In other words there are interdependent utility functions. Another explanation is that education provides external benefits to

Group B. These externalities, however, are never specified very precisely, and there is a dearth of supporting evidence. Usually writers confine themselves to a *presumption* that they exist and give one or two possible illustrations. The most popular example is that an "educated" child will be more law-abiding. This assumption has been examined empirically elsewhere[22] and it has been shown that the evidence does not support it. In any case the idea has always seemed ambiguous. If a member of a neighboring family invades or damages my property, I normally look to the law for compensation. It is held in the present instance, however, that I should compensate the potential trespassers with school subsidies in the hope that this will reduce the probability of their damaging me. This seems a curious external *benefit*.

Instead of naked coercion, let us now examine the "constitutional approach." Each individual is treated as a choicemaker in his selection from basic sets of legal frameworks. Every individual is now a decision-maker not only in the market place and at the ballot-box but also in the setting up of the basic constitution which lays down the ground rules within the chosen democratic system. Imagine a new community settlement of young immigrant adults where no children have yet been born and no constitution has yet been laid down. Each adult will now have to consider not only his future private utility of having children but also the potential disutility from the "undesirable" behavior or appearance of the neighbor's children. Since the neighbor will be in the reverse position (fearing the potential disutility from one's own children) a constitutional rule may be agreed to, laying down the conditions in which the "privileges of parenthood" shall be conferred. One of these conditions will be that each parent will supply a given minimum of education, food, clothing, and so on, from his own resources. If society depends exclusively on these conditions to protect children and to provide sufficient external benefits, then no subsidies, income transfers, or price reductions will be necessary for any of the goods and services mentioned. Because of the anticipated legal responsibilities, adults will be discouraged from marriage or parenthood until they can afford to bring their children up in conformity with the minimum constitutional standards. Pareto's "optimality" will now be achieved by a preliminary and unanimous agreement to abide by the chosen democratic rules. Compulsion will still be a principle in schooling, but it will be compulsion of parents to purchase schooling, like other necessities, in the upbringing of their children. Schooling will be positively priced.

The community could of course also choose to have a "second line of defense" in the form of occasional subsidies or income transfers to meet the needs of marginal (insurance-type) cases, such as those where families become suddenly destitute. Clearly we have now isolated two polar cases. The first is the circumstance of constitutional compulsion where the adult is previously contracted to full responsibility for prerequisite levels of consumption of externality-generating goods. The second is the opposite where the community accepts full responsibility and supplies these goods free of charge together with compensatory income transfers where necessary. In the second case, "compulsion" is of an emasculated kind.

Does this "constitutional explanation" hold good? Conceptually there is a problem of infinite regress—of knowing which individual preferences to respect: those at the constitutional stage or those where the individual wants to rebel at some subsequent period. Again in the real world we observe piecemeal plans and a combination of devices. While families are expected to clothe their children adequately, children's apparel is not, as is schooling, made free to all; neither are there (with respect to clothing) any universally compulsory laws fully equivalent to those related to schooling. True, there are "child abuse" laws requiring minimum standards of consumption of food and clothing. As distinct from the way schooling is customarily provided, however, no financial benefits exist to supplement the operation of these laws directly although welfare or child assistance subsidies probably have that effect. Nor are there specific subsidies for the housing of children. Parents expect that they have to face obligations to purchase food for their offspring at positive prices. School lunches are often subsidized, it is true, but rarely are they so fully subsidized as to allow consumers to enjoy zero prices. School lunches, moreover, are not subsidized on non-school days. It is evident that some rough conformity with the polar cases or normative welfare principles previously outlined does appear here and there. The principles upon which mixtures of these cases appear are, however, quite obscure.

We come back to the fact that the real world contains far from "perfect" political processes. This being so, the constitutional dimension of our problem merges once more with the economics of politics or in this case "imperfect" politics. Vote-gaining behavior in an oligopolistic political structure could well be of significant explanatory value. An extension of compulsion may improve the image of a political party even though few individual families suffer disutility. By anticipating future national income increases, a government may announce plans for raising the compulsory school period years ahead. In doing so, it need antagonize very few, since, to repeat, compulsion may simply underline what most people would do anyway.

We have to return to the 1870s in England to discover the circumstances in which these important issues were openly confronted. Helena Fawcett and her husband, Henry Fawcett, Professor of Political Economy at Cambridge,[23] both represented what we have called the constitutional view. They both strongly urged compulsion but threw down the challenge that if schooling was to be made free, so too should food and clothing. If free schooling was to be adopted, they insisted, it should be openly acknowledged to be another form of relief; and the danger should be faced that, like free food and clothing, free schooling would eventually pauperize the whole community. Sir Charles Dilke, spokesman for the "non-constitutionalists" in the Birmingham League (the pressure group for compulsory, free and non-sectarian schooling), took strong objection. Helena Fawcett's reasoning, he argued, was the "*reductio ad absurdum* of some of the oldest principles of science to degrade the people in order to maintain an economic theory."[24] The analogy between free schooling and free food was a false one, Dilke said. Intervention to save a child from starvation was a justifiable protection of an *individual*—protection of an individual member of society who was incapable of protecting himself. Free and compulsory schooling, on the other hand, was justifiable because it protected the society. "The state suffers by crime and outrage, the results of ignorance. It interferes, therefore, to protect itself."[25] This identification of the poor sections of society with the criminal class was widespread among the Victorian gentility. Dilke and his associates in the Birmingham League did not consider for one moment the possibility that they also (like Mrs. Fawcett) were "degrading the people in order to maintain an economic theory."[26]

In addition to the crime reduction argument, free and compulsory schooling was connected with the need for national defense. As Dilke put it:

> ...education comes far nearer to drill than it does to clothes. Drill, or compulsory service of all citizens in time of emergency, may become a state necessity.[27]

The military success of Prussia against France in 1870 was clearly uppermost in their minds. Jesse Collins, the secretary of the Birmingham League, echoed Dilke's sentiments:

> ...the policy of the country on critical occasions, involving war or any other calamity, has to be determined by the people, and it is of the greatest national importance that they should be fitted by education to exercise an intelligent judgment on any subject submitted to their decision....all are taxed for the maintenance of the army, navy, and police, because all share in the benefits these institutions are supposed to afford, and would have to share in the loss and inconvenience resulting from their non-existence; and by the same rule all should be taxed for the support of schools because all share in the increased wealth, security, and general advantages resulting from the education of the people, and have also to share the expense and danger of crime and other results of ignorance.[28]

The argument so far, however, had not really destroyed the analogy of schooling with food and clothing. A half-starved, half-clad population would be just as useless in defense as a half-educated one. Joseph Chamberlain added another argument that seemed more consistent. Food was a necessity for existence, but schooling was not a necessity at all:

> Human nature, which was almost perpetually hungry, might be trusted to supply itself with the elements of bare existence; but human nature could not be trusted to supply itself with instruction, of which a great many human beings had, unfortunately, a very low opinion.[29]

One missing element in Chamberlain's theory was attention to the problem of how such an "irreponsible" population could be relied upon to vote for politicians like himself who wanted to regiment them, now that democracy had largely arrived (with 1867 enfranchisement). It was not just a question of "educating our masters"; there was the problem of politically persuading the "masters" to elect their mentors. Chamberlain imputed irresponsibility to "a great many human beings." A great many more, indeed the majority of families, had proved that they did have a high opinion of schooling. In 1869 most parents were buying it directly, most families were already sending their children to school without being compelled, most school leavers were literate, and most of "our masters," in other words, were already being educated of their own free will.[30] The argument for compulsion applied at most to only a small minority of families.

But the Birmingham League supporters meant something more in their arguments. The "human nature" that "would not be trusted to supply itself with instruction" was really at fault because it could not supply itself with the *right sort of instruction*. It had allowed itself to be given a schooling that was connected with religious organizations—especially of Anglican persuasion. The Birmingham League was an expression of the newer secular nationalism of the nineteenth century. It included many whom the twentieth century could now describe as "false optimists." The system of compulsion they had in mind included compelling people to change from sectarian to secular (or non-sectarian) schools. They knew that this could not be accomplished by direct means; other groups had to be reckoned with—High Tories, for instance, believed that only a school controlled by the established church could be effective in improving morality and decreasing crime. The methods adopted by the league involved the strategic use of the new "board schools" that were established by the Education Act of 1870 to fill gaps in the voluntary system of denominational and other private schools. Soon after 1870 these new institutions, which were largely non-sectarian if not secular, were beginning to price many of the church schools out of the field. This was a consequence of the board schools' ability to draw heavily upon the "rates" (local property taxes) and so survive and win any competition. Church schools, the league argued, should not be supported by the "rates," because that would involve the objectionable practice of subsidizing religions. People should pay for their religious instruction separately.

In 1875, the Reverend F. S. Dale spoke up against the campaign of the Birmingham League for universally free schools. He did not oppose the *selective* remission of burdens upon the poor but complained that the league's desire for *universally* free schooling (in the new board schools) was a desire to undermine the 1870 Education Act and destroy existing schools. "Free schools were part of yet a greater scheme, when the Church of England should be thrown over."[31] Jesse Collins, in behalf of the league, made the following candid reply (here in reported speech):

> With regard to Mr. F. S. Dale's assertion that the free system would close the voluntary schools—denominational

schools was the best name—he quite admitted, and he thought they ought not to deny, that, in so far as they were sectarian institutions, or remained for sectarian purposes, the free system would kill them. It was the pure Darwinian theory—the fittest only would survive. If education was the object, then the free scheme got them out of all their difficulties, because they could not deny that by the free system under the school board, a better education would be given than could possibly be given by the voluntary schools, on account of their precarious income....[32]

Edwin Chadwick also supported compulsory attendance provided it was at the right (i.e., the "nationalized") schools. He complained that the small sectarian schools did not provide the appropriate secular curriculum: "The experience is now accumulating of the great disadvantages of the small separate schools." In the large schools subsidized or established or controlled by governments there were the "superior" attractions of "gymnastic exercises, the drill, elementary drawing, music, *military fetes* and parades, to which the small sectarian could not obtain...."[33]

Clearly this survey has brought the special circumstances of politics well into the picture. From simple normative economics it *is* conceivable that the public might vote to live under a constitution that provides compulsory, free, and secular schools that are primarily designed to insure military protection and domestic order. Each individual will then express his own preferences *ex ante*. It is arguable that, *ex post*, compulsion could thus be reconciled with the tradition of respect for individual preference that the welfare economics of Pareto endorses. The argument depends, however, on unanimous or near-unanimous consent. The most elementary reference to the historical record encourages doubt whether there was anything like a popularly articulated preference for the system that evolved. The positive economics of politics (especially the politics of pressure groups) seems to explain more than the normative economics of voluntary constitutions.

It has been shown that historically compulsion in Britain was closely interrelated with the issue of "free" schooling. Both compulsion and free provision were introduced in such special ways as to suggest that the general public were more manipulated than consulted. There is in fact no known English record of direct consultation of individual families to discover their wishes in the late nineteenth century. There *is* such a record concerning their views as to the desirability of "free" education. This was contained in the intensive nineteenth century survey of education by the Newcastle Commission. It reported in 1861:

> Almost all the evidence goes to show that though the offer of gratuitous education might be accepted by a certain proportion of the parents, it would in general be otherwise. The sentiment of independence is strong, and it is wounded by the offer of an absolutely gratuitous education.[34]

Such evidence was not good enough for Jesse Collins, the enthusiast and propagandist for America-type common schools, and secretary of the Birmingham League pressure group that eventually had such important influence. It will be fitting to conclude with the sentiments he expressed on the eve of the league's establishment:

> It is frequently urged that the public mind is not yet ripe for such laws as free public schools would necessitate, and that it is unwise to legislate so much in advance of public opinion. The public mind is more easily led in a right direction than government sometimes wish it to be, and in

> this instance, if fairly tested would probably be found ful-
> ly under the idea of a national system of compulsory, un-
> sectarian education...and this reveals the necessity for
> the immediate formation of a society, national in its name
> and constitution, refusing all compromise, but adopting as
> its platform—*national, secular (or unsectarian) education,*
> *compulsory as to rating and attendance, with state aid*
> *and inspection, and local management.* The action of
> such a society would be similar to that of the Anti-Corn
> Law League, and its success as certain; by lectures, by
> writing, by agitation in every town, it would give direction
> and voice to the fresh and ever-increasing interest felt by
> the people in this matter.[35]

Whether "fresh and ever-increasing interest" was
eventually felt by the people has never been demonstrated. Certainly the politicians did find voters to support
their programs of free and compulsory "education," but
that is not necessarily the same thing. Compulsion in
"education" can mean many things and can be applied
in several ways and with a variety of consequences. The
strongest nineteenth-century motivation behind the politically expressed "need" for compulsion in Britain was
a desire to compel the majority to secularize their "education." To do this, compulsion had to be what we shall
describe (for want of a better word) as "universal compulsion." This denotes an "ambitious," consciously decided, or comprehensive piece of legislation that is
embodied in a statute about compulsion *per se*. We shall
distinguish this from the type of compulsion that is
usually implicit in ordinary child-abuse laws that attempt
to deal with cases on a more *ad hoc* basis. Such provision we have called "selective compulsion."

"Selective" compulsion could certainly meet problems
caused by a minority of delinquents or poor families;
but this would not reduce the power of the church and

the free choice of schools by the majority of parents. Reduced parental choice in fact, to repeat, was the consequence of "universal" compulsion because it was coupled with a policy of making the schools "free." Free choice was curtailed because only secular schools qualified to be "free."

"Selective" compulsion can be a constructive, proper, and humane provision in society. To many who support this idea, however, "universal" compulsion, as described above, will have indirect costs that are so severe as to outweigh the benefits. Modern political circumstances nevertheless seem unconducive to these sentiments. It may be, as Jesse Collins believed, that the "public mind" is more easily led than most people think. And this could be more likely after a hundred years of uniform "education" in compulsory public schools.

NOTES

[1] *Parliamentary Papers*, 1841, Vol. X.

[2] *Principles*, 1909, Ashley Edition, p. 954.

[3] *Ibid.*, p. 955.

[4] *Ibid.*, p. 953.

[5] I.e., sales volume rises with disposable income. Example: entertainment and travel. Example of *zero* income elasticity of demand might be common salt.—*Ed.*

[6] *Ibid.*, Section IV.

[7] *New York Times*, February 12, 1970, p. 1. Quoted by Barry Chiswick, "Minimum Schooling Legislation, Externalities and a 'Child Tax,' " *Journal of Law and Economics*, 1972 (forthcoming).

[8]Joseph Chamberlain, "Six Years of Educational Work in Birmingham," an address delivered to the Birmingham School Board, November 2, 1876, pp. 19-20.

[9]The following illustration and parts of the subsequent argument are taken from my *Economical Education and the Politician*. Institute of Econ. Affairs, Hobart Paper 42, London, 1968. This work develops the argument especially in the context of the forthcoming raising of annual leaving age in Britain.

[10]E. G. West, "The Political Economy of American Public School Legislation," *Journal of Law & Economics*, 1967.

[11]*Ibid.*, p. 124.

[12]*Ibid.*, p. 124.

[13]W. M. Landes and L. C. Solmon, "Compulsory Schooling Legislation: An economic Analysis of the Law and Social Change in the Nineteenth Century." *Journal of Economic History*, March 1972.

[14]See especially the annual reports to the Education Department of W. J. Kennedy (1872), Mr. Waddington (1872), Mr. Bowstead (1871), Rev. F. Watkins (1872), Rev. F. F. Cornish (1882), J. G. Fitch (1882), G. H. Gordon (1882).

[15]Matthew Arnold's Report for 1867.

[16]*Op. cit.*

[17]Mr. Bowstead's General Report for 1871.

[18]Annual Report of the New York Superintendent of Public Instruction, 1871.

[19]*15 to 18, A Report of the Central Advisory Council for Education (England), 1959,* Para. 100.

[20]W. Hansen, B. A. Weisbrod, and W. Scanlon, "Schooling and Earnings of Low Achievers," *AER*, Vol. LX, No. 3, June 1970, p. 417. See also the subsequent comments by Barry Chiswick, Stanley Masters, and Thomas Ribich, and the reply

by Hansen et al., *AER*, Vol. LXII, No. 4, September 1972, p. 752.

[21] For further details see E. G. West, "Subsidized But Compulsory Consumption Goods: Some Special Cases," *Kyklos*, 1971.

[22] E. G. West, *Education and the State*, second edition, 1970, Ch. 3.

[23] He was Alfred Marshall's predecessor in the Cambridge chair.

[24] Sir Charles Dilke, Report of the Third Annual Meeting of the National Educational League held in Birmingham, October 17th and 18th 1871.

[25] *Ibid.*

[26] Dilke's arguments were repeated especially by Joseph Chamberlain, Jesse Collins, and Edwin Chadwick.

[27] *Ibid.*, p. 157.

[28] Jesse Collins, *Remarks on the Establishment of Common Schools in England,* 1872.

[29] Joseph Chamberlain, "Free Schools" address to the Birmingham School Board, June 18th, 1875.

[30] Most people still find these facts surprising. Yet they are facts; and they have been obscured by years of "official" and "quasi-official" histories of education. See E. G. West, *Education and the State*, 2nd ed. 1970. Also *Education and Industrial Revolution*, Batsford, London.

[31] Meeting of the Birmingham School Board, June 18th, 1875.

[32] *Ibid.* The "survival of the fittest" analogy was obscure; in the Darwinian scheme it was not a matter of subsidized animals surviving the non-subsidized, or the heavily subsidized surviving the weakly subsidized.

[33] Edwin Chadwick, "National Education: A letter thereon to the Lord President of the Council," 1870.

[34]1861 Report, Vol. I, page 73.

[35]Written in 1867, this passage is contained in Jesse Collins, *Remarks on the Establishment of Common Schools in England*. 1872, pages 46-47. The italics are in the original.

Barry Chiswick, *op. cit.*

William H. Branson, "Social Legislation and the Birth Rate in C19th Britain," *Western Economic Journal*, March 1968.

Branson, *op. cit.*, argues this case.

G. Balfour, *The Educational Systems of Great Britain & Ireland*, Oxford 1898.

Legal Bibliography

(The Law as It Relates to Compulsory Education and Schooling)

I—Legal Cases

II—Books

III—Articles

Annotated and Compiled by

Robert P. Baker (I) and H. George Resch (II and III)

I—Legal Cases

The following listing is intended to be selective rather than exhaustive. It is a compilation of judicial opinions only, from which the legal scholar can enter the field of contemporary compulsory education law. The annotations represent the opinions of the compiler.

1   Abington School District v. Schempp, 374 U.S. 203 (1963).
The famous case in which the United States Supreme Court held that compulsory Bible-reading in public schools violates the First Amendment.

2   Alford v. Board of Education, 298 Ky. 803, 184 S.W.2d 207 (1944).

Holding that failure of a school board to provide safe transportation for pupils in accordance with statute exempts parents from compliance with compulsory education law.

3   Anderson v. State, 84 Ga. App. 259, 65 S.E.2d 848 (1951).

A vaccination controversy, supporting the proposition that a parent must not only send a child to school, but must also prepare the child in such a manner as to assure his admittance.

4   Beiler, Commonwealth v., 168 Pa. Super. 462, 79 A.2d 134 (1951).

One of a series (see Nos. 28 and 33) illustrating the problems of the Amish when public officials are antagonistic.

5   Bey, Commonwealth v., 166 Pa. Super. 136, 70 A.2d 693 (1950).

Holding that religious convictions, requiring regular and repeated absences from public school, cannot justify parents in violating compulsory education statute's demand for attendance every school day.

6   Chalfin, State *ex rel.*, v. Glick, 113 Ohio App. 23, 177 N.E.2d 293 (1960), *aff'd*, 172 Ohio St. 249, 175 N.E.2d 68 (1961).

Illustrating extra-legal attempts by public officials to persecute Amish operating their own schools.

7   Crouse, *ex parte*, 54 Pa. (4 Whart.) 9, 11 (1839).

The earliest judicial expression of the collectivist precept that education is a societal rather than a parental function. Widely cited and concurred in later.

8   Cumming v. Richmond County Board of Education, 175 U.S. 528 (1899).

Holding that public education is solely a matter of state law, in which federal interference can be justified only if a right established under the Constitution is imperilled.

9   Dobbins v. Commonwealth, 198 Va. 697, 96 S.E.2d 154 (1957).

Compulsory education law may not be employed as a threat to induce a citizen to forgo the exercise of his Constitutional rights. Refusal to submit to segregated schooling is justifiable. See also no. 32.

10   Donahoe v. Richards, 38 Me. 376 (1854).

Earliest judicial justification of forcing Protestant Bible upon Catholic children in the public schools. See also nos. 38 and 1, in that order, for erosion of this attitude over the years.

11   Engel v. Vitale, 370 U.S. 421 (1962).

Holding that it is no part of the function of any government agency or official to prescribe prayers for anyone, and that such prayers in the classroom, having the authority of government behind them, violate the First Amendment.

12   Fish, People *ex rel.*, v. Sandstrom, 167 Misc. 436, 3 N.Y.S.2d 1006 (Suffolk County Ct. 1938), *rev'd*, 279 N.Y. 523, 18 N.E.2d 840, 7 N.Y.S.2d 523 (1939).

Flag-salute case, illustrating principle that parents are not to be held responsible for refusal of child to comply with school regulations, and that violation of compulsory education statute cannot be sustained in the absence of proof of wrongful intent (minority rule).

13   Garber, State v., 197 Kan. 567, 419 P.2d 896 (1966), *cert. denied*, 389 U.S. 51 (1967).

Arising out of legislative attempt to force Amish "into mainstream of American life." Tragic case of religious persecution and judicial disregard of settled law. See also nos. 30 and 41.

14   Gault, *In re*, 387 U.S. 1 (1967).

Holding that Fourteenth Amendment guarantees of due process apply to children as well as to adults. Clearest and most authoritative judicial recognition of children's Constitutional rights.

15   Hershberger, *In re*, no. 2835 (Wayne County Juv. Ct. 1958), *aff'd, sub nom.* State v. Hershberger, 77 Ohio L. Abs. 487, 150 N.E.2d 671 (Wayne County Juv. Ct. 1958), *rev'd, per curium*, 83 Ohio L. Abs. 62, 168 N.E.2d 13 (App. Ct. Wayne County 1959).

Almost incredible official and judicial persecution of an Amishman, who was ultimately vindicated.

16   King, People *ex rel.*, v. Gallagher, 93 N.Y. 438 (1833).

Early case of statist attitude toward education, justifying racial discrimination on the ground that the state may order "its" school system in any manner it may please. Profitably read in conjunction with no. 35.

17   Knox v. O'Brien, 7 N.J. Super. 608, 72 A.2d 389 (Cape May County Ct., L. Div. 1950).

Second in a trio of cases showing the imposition by judicial fiat, in disregard of statute, of a "cookie-cutter" philosophy of education. Foreshadowed in no. 34 and ultimately rejected in no. 21.

18   Levisen, People v., 404 Ill. 574, 90 N.E.2d 213 (1950).

Penetrating, enlightened opinion, typical of recent judicial attitude toward compulsory education in Illinois, upholding right of parent to educate child personally at home, despite absence of specific statutory provision. Profitably compared to no. 31.

19   Lewis, People *ex rel.*, v. Graves, 127 Misc. 135, 215 N.Y.S. 632 (Sup. Ct. 1926), *aff'd*, 245 N.Y. 195, 156 N.E. 663 (1927).

One of many actions instituted by the late militant atheist, Joseph Lewis, drawing a distinction between irregular attendance, constituting grounds for disciplinary action, and mere occasional absence, requiring only a reasonable excuse. The power to distinguish between the two is vested in local school boards. Compare with no. 5.

20   Marsh's Case, 140 Pa. Super. 472, 14 A.2d 368 (1940).

The last in a series of cases (the others are cited in this report) illustrating the futility of criminal sanctions for violation of compulsory education laws, particularly when recalcitrance is founded upon religious convictions.

21 Massa, State v., 95 N.J. Super. 382, 231 A.2d 252 (Morris County Ct., L. Div. 1950).

Last of a trio of cases (see also nos. 34 and 17) illustrating the imposition and, in this case, the ultimate overthrow of the "cookie-cutter" theory of compulsory education.

22 Miday, State v., 263 N.C. 747, 140 S.E.2d 325 (1965).

Illustrating the minority, more liberal, rules in dealing with religious objections to innoculation as a prerequisite to admission to public school. Also illustrative of procedural niceties involved in criminal prosecutions for compulsory education violations. Compare to no. 3.

23 Minor, Board of Education v., 23 Ohio St. 211 (1872).

A ringing defense of individual rights in one of the earliest Bible-reading cases. "Government is an organization for particular purposes. It is not almighty, and we are not to look to it for everything." Compare to attitude of dissenters in no. 38.

24 Morton v. Board of Education, 69 Ill. App. 2d 38, 216 N.E.2d 305 (1966).

Upholding "dual enrolment" plan, whereby compulsory education law is satisfied through part-time public school attendance, plus additional attendance at educational institution of parents' choice. See also, no. 18.

25 Mountain Lakes Board of Education v. Maas, 56 N.J. Super. 245, 152 A.2d 394 (App. Div. 1959), *aff'd*, 31 N.J. 537, 158 A.2d 330, *cert. denied*, 363 U.S. 843 (1960).

Protracted and complex struggle over inoculation as prerequisite to public school admittance. Extensive discussion by courts of the history and present state of the law in this regard. A leading case. See also and compare nos. 20 and 22.

26 Nebel v. Nebel, 99 N.J. Super. 256, 239 A.2d 266 (Ch. Div. 1968), *aff'd*, 103 N.J. Super. 216, 247 A.2d 27 (App. Div. 1968).

Divorce case involving education expenses of child. Reviews, reaffirms, and for the first time implements by force of law the proposition underlying the present American compulsory education laws—that a parent is obligated to educate a child. Compare this case to older no. 29, demonstrating development of this theory.

27 Pierce v. Society of Sisters, 268 U.S. 510 (1925).

Without doubt the most famous case dealing with schools in the history of American jurisprudence, this case established the right of private schools to exist and of parents to discharge their obligations under the compulsory education laws through such schools. It has been almost universally and by now irretrievably misunderstood as holding that compulsory education laws are unassailable under the federal constitution, a question not involved in the case. Compare nos. 28 and 40.

28 Petersheim, Commonwealth v., 70 Pa. D. & C. 432 (Somerset County Ct. 1949), *aff'd*. 166 Pa. Super. 90, 70 A.2d 395 (1950).

Unusual case, lower court relying upon *Pierce* (no. 27) to hold compulsory education statute unconstitutional as applied to Amish. Appellate court affirmed acquittal of particular defendant, avoiding double jeopardy possibility, but indicated—also relying upon *Pierce*!—that there was no constitutional bar, thus paving the way for further persecution of Amish illustrated in nos. 4 and 33. See ultimate vindication of Amish in no. 41.

29 Purse, Board of Education v., 101 Ga. 422, 28 S.E. 896 (1897).

Early authority supporting parent-benefit theory of public education. Public schools exist to permit discharge of parental obligation, not to benefit children directly. Arguably, the case yet stands for good law in some jurisdictions. Compare judicial attitude in no. 7.

30 Sherbert v. Verner, 374 U.S. 398 (1963).

The principle established in this somewhat neglected case

was employed by the Wisconsin Supreme Court to rule compulsory education unconstitutional as applied to the Amish (see no. 41): State action indirectly infringing upon religious liberty cannot be justified by mere power of the state to regulate generally the activities in question, but only by the necessity of regulating without exception.

31   Shoreline, State *ex rel.*, v. Superior Court, 55 Wash 2d 177, 346 P.2d 999 (1959), *cert. denied*, 363 U.S. 814 (1960).

Probably the most striking example in American jurisprudence of statism running rampant over individual rights regarding education of children. A 5-4 decision, with a blistering dissent, holding that Washington parents may not personally educate their children at home if they do not hold state teacher's certificate, despite the absence of any such requirement in the pertinent statute and despite a judicial finding that the education provided is at least equivalent to that provided by the public schools. Profitably read in conjunction with no. 18, illustrating a more reasonable attitude.

32   Skipwith, *In re*, 14 Misc.2d 325, 180 N.Y.S.2d 852 (N.Y. City Dom. Rel. Ct., Child. Ct. Div. 1958).

Illustrating extreme limits of judicial thought in regard to discrimination and compulsory education: "These parents have the constitutionally guaranteed right to elect no education for their children rather than to subject them to discriminatorily inferior education." Compare this attitude with that prevailing earlier in the same jurisdiction, no. 16.

33   Smoker, Commonwealth v., 177 Pa. Super. 435, 110 A.2d 740 (1955).

Last in a trio of cases (see nos. 28 and 4) demonstrating the erosion of statutory guarantees to Amish through judicial encroachment.

34   Stephens v. Bongart, 15 N.J. Misc. 80, 189 A. 131 (Juv. & Dom. Rel. Ct. 1937).

First in a series of cases showing the imposition of the "cookie-cutter" theory of public education through judicial fiat in defiance of statute. See also nos. 17 and 21.

35   Stoutmeyer, State *ex rel.*, v. Duffy, 7 Nev. 342 (1872).

A case, almost a century before the famous Brown v. Board of Education, holding that racially segregated public school system was repugnant to the Nevada Constitution. Contrast judicial attitude in no. 16.

36   Troyer v. State, 29 Ohio Dec. 168, 21 Ohio N.P. 121 (Logan C.P. 1918).

The earliest reported flag-salute case, holding that refusal to salute justifies expulsion. Opinion is notable for vituperation and jingoism. Contrast with no. 39.

37   Turner, People v., 121 Cal. App. 2d 861, 263 P.2d 685 (App. Dep't, Super. Ct. 1953).

Case establishing discrimination against parents teaching their own children at home in favor of teachers in private schools. The former are required to be state-certified, while the latter are not. Example of justifying violation of rights on the basis of administrative expediency.

38   Vollmar, People *ex rel.*, v. Stanley, 81 Colo. 276, 255 P. 610 (1927).

Bible-reading case, treated as dispute over curriculum. Established principle in Colorado that parent may make a reasonable choice for his child among courses offered by public school. Profitably read in conjunction with nos. 10 and 23.

39   West Virginia State Board of Education v. Barnette, 319 U.S. 624 (1943).

Established rule that school officials may not coerce students to salute flag or recite any pledge. One of the most famous Jehovah's Witnesses constitutional cases.

40   Williams, State v., 56 S.D. 370, 228 N.W. 470 (1929).

Only case in which the highest court of any American jurisdiction was squarely faced with the necessity of deciding upon the constitutionality of compulsory education. Relying upon the *Pierce* dictum (no. 27), the South Dakota court held that compulsory education is constitutional.

41   Yoder, State v., 49 Wis. 2d 430, 182 N.W.2d 539 (1971), *aff'd*, 32 L. Ed.2d 15 (1972).

Vindication of Amish contention that compulsory education laws, as applied to them, unconstitutionally infringe upon religious liberty, where law would require schooling in non-Amish milieu above the elementary level. U.S. Supreme Court affirmation appears unduly restrictive and rule of this case is likely to be extended. Profitably read in conjunction with no. 13.

42   Gonyaw v. Gray, 361 F. Supp. 366 (D. Vt. 1967).

In Vermont, *any* degree of corporal punishment inflicted upon a pupil by a teacher is constitutionally permissible, if the punishment is "reasonable."

43   Holmes v. Nestor, 81 Ariz 372, 306 P.2d 290 (S. Ct. Ariz. 1968).

Attendance officer may, without warrant, take into custody any child subject to compulsory attendance law.

44   Meinhold v. Taylor, cert. den., mem., 38 L. Ed.2d 167 (S. Ct. U. S. 1973).

United States Supreme Court declines to review holding of Nevada Supreme Court that a teacher may be discharged for being in disagreement with compulsory education law and expressing such opinions, although no pupil was advised to break law; blistering dissent by Justice Douglas.

45   Peacock v. Riggsbee, 309 F. Supp. 542 (D. Ga. 1970).

Reaffirming principle that there is no federal constitutional right to a public education.

46   Valent v. New Jersey State Board of Education, 118 N.J. Supper 416, 288 A.2d 52 (App. Div. 1970).

On parent's right to reject part of curriculum for child—sex education courses.

47   Woods v. Wright, 334 F.2d 369 (5th Cir. Ala. 1962).

State may not employ truancy laws as a means of racial discrimination.

II—Books

Bender, John Frederick. *The Functions of Courts in Enforcing School Attendance Laws*, New York: Teacher's College, Columbia University Press, 1927.

Drury, Robert L. and Ray, Kenneth C. "Compulsory Attendance," in *Essentials of School Law*, New York: Appleton-Century-Crofts, 1967.

Edwards, Newton. *The Courts and the Public Schools: The Legal Basis of School Organization and Administration*. Chicago: University of Chicago Press, 1955.

Hamilton, Robert and Mort, Paul R. *The Law and Public Education*. Chicago: The Foundation Press, 1941.

Johnson, George M. *Education Law*. East Lansing, Mich.: Michigan State University Press, 1969.

Reuther, E. Edmind, Jr. and Hamilton, Robert R. *The Law of Public Education*. Mineola, N.Y.: Foundation Press, 1970.

Rogers, Harrell R. *Community Conflict, Public Opinion, and the Law: The Amish Dispute in Iowa*. Columbus, Ohio: Merrill Publishing Co., 1969.

Spurlock, Clark. *Education and the Supreme Court*. Urbana, Ill.: University of Illinois Press, 1955.

III—Articles

Arons, Stephen. "Compulsory Education—The Plain People Resist." *The Saturday Review*, January 1972, pp. 52-57.
Stephen Arons considers the Supreme Court case of Wisconsin v. Yoder. Admittedly the legal question is the quite narrow one of religious freedom. Mr. Arons claims that the case, despite the narrowness of the legal decision, does call into question the entire rationale for compulsory schooling.

Baker, Helen. "Crack in Liberty Bell: Compulsory Education,"
   Civil Liberties, April 1972, p. 1.

   In this eloquent plea for educational freedom, the author
   contends that "the school systems of America are the single largest state agency for the deprivation of rights, start-
   ing at an early age and on a captive audience." Among
   these deprivations are "denial of free speech, free press,
   and free association; denial of religious freedom; denial
   of due process, including punishment without a hearing
   and denial of the right to remain silent; cruel and unusual punishment; suspension and expulsion used as harass-
   ment; selective punishment; invasion of privacy and so
   on." The most fundamental deprivation, however, is the
   denial of a right to an education.

   The author urges the ACLU to challenge the compulsory attendance laws on the grounds that "we believe the
   right to an education is so basic that unless there is some
   way to challenge the monolithic structure of compulsory
   institutionalization, all liberty will be lost. Let us say that
   the indictment shows that most schools do not educate...and that the compulsory school community is essentially not a learning environment."

Baker, Robert P. "Compulsory Education in the United States:
   Big Brother Goes to School. *"Seton Hall Law Review* 3
   (1972): 349-385.

   Have compulsory education laws tended to undermine
   the corresponding parental right to education of the
   child? What conflicts exist between individual rights and
   laws in the field of education? What has been the goal of
   compulsory education legislation? Are we closer to or far-
   ther from that goal? Do compulsory education laws, as
   they now exist and are applied, complement the rights of
   children and their parents?

   These are the fundamental questions that Mr. Baker
   asks to begin his analysis. He attempts a comprehensive
   survey of all legislation related to the issue of where

rights reside and have resided when it comes to educating the child.

Mr. Baker criticizes compulsory education laws for being penal in nature, restrictive as to the manner in which parents discharge their obligation, and often detrimental to the rights of the child.

Caston, Frances. "Is There a Right Not to Go to School?" *Scholastic Teacher* (October, 1972): 20-24.

The author presents a view of the operation of the compulsory education laws as seen by the truant officers charged with their enforcement.

While he is basically sympathetic to such legislation, he feels that such laws could profitably be modified to allow for greater flexibility. He points out that a recent NEA Task Force on compulsory education said that "all Americans require an education, but not necessarily 6 hours a day, 30 hours a week, 36 weeks a year in a building called 'school.' The Task Force recommended a flexible school timetable and urged the adoption of amendments to compulsory attendance laws which would give individual schools and school systems the option to develop alternative programs to the present ones requiring specific periods of time in school buildings."

Gardner, G. K. "Liberty, The State, and the School," *Catholic Law* 1 (1955): 285 ff.

Haight, J. T. "The Amish School Controversy," *Ohio Bar* 31 (1958): 846 ff.

Hiser, P. N. "Compulsory Education in Relation to the Charity Problem," In *Conference of Charities and Corrections,* N.Y., 1900.

Written at a time when compulsory attendance laws were just beginning to be enforced in earnest. The author, who was head truant officer for the City of Indianapolis, points out a number of practical difficulties in their enforcement. The difficulties he enumerates remain today, and continue to make effective enforcement of such laws all but impossible.

Johnson, A. C., Jr. "Our Schools Make Criminals," *Journal of Criminal Law* 33 (1942): 310-315.

"The Right Not to be Modern Men: The Amish and Compulsory Education," *Virginia Law Review* 53 (1967): 925 ff.

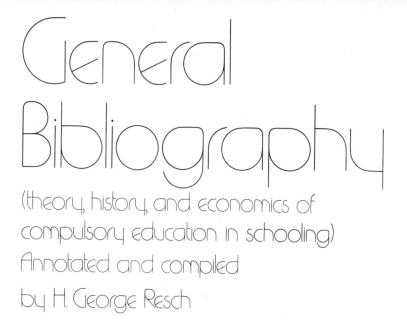

General Bibliography

(theory, history, and economics of compulsory education in schooling)
Annotated and compiled
by H. George Resch

I—Books

Adams, Paul, and others. *Children's Rights: Toward the Liberation of the Child*. London: Elek, 1971.

> Collection of essays advocating greater autonomy for children.
>
> One of the authors (Nan Berger) points out that "the present law which makes it compulsory for a child to attend school between the ages of five and fifteen does little to enhance the status of children or lead them to a self-regulating life. Compulsion of this kind would be totally unacceptable for adults in the so-called free world. Why should it be acceptable in relation to children?...In fact compulsory education is the beginning of the conditioning of the individual to the unquestioning obedience on which an authoritarian state depends. No conscientious objection is allowed; no pay award made for work done; submission to the school hierarchy is demanded; infringement of school discipline and absenteeism are punished."

Has useful bibliography of books critical of educational establishment.

Association for Christian Schools. *Schools Weighed in the Balance*. Houston: St. Thomas Press, 1962.

This brief study is a defense of private, voluntary education. The author maintains that by virtue of its compulsory support and compulsory attendance American schooling "is synonymous with politics in the worst sense of the word.... the politicizing of education means the perversion of education, the fostering of community strife and social disintegration, and ultimately the imposition of totalitarian solutions."

Bell, Sadie. *The Church, The State and Education in Virginia, 1930*. New York: Arno Press, 1972.

Useful in that it shows the extent of the educational efforts conducted by the various religious denominations prior to the advent of compulsory schooling in Virginia.

Berg, Ivar. *Education and Jobs: The Great Training Robbery*. Boston: Beacon Press, 1971

Argues that we have tended to overrate the importance of the amount of schooling to job performance, and concludes that "in every instance, the data prove overwhelmingly that the critical determinants of performance are not increased educational achievement but other personality characteristics and environmental conditions."

Billings, Thomas Arthur. *The Old Order Amish Versus the Compulsory Attendance Laws: An Analysis of the Conflict*. (Microfilm, Ph.D. dissertation, University of Oregon, 1961).

An overall treatment of the continuing struggle between the Amish and the advocates of compulsory state schooling. The author takes his stand "on grounds of religious principle, moral law, and the constitution, for individual liberty, for religious freedom, for parental rights to educate their children, and against state tyranny and intervention in an individual's affairs."

Dennison, George. *The Lives of Children: The Story of the First Street School.* New York: Random House, 1970.

Highly personal account of this famous American "free school." In commenting on the impact this school had on the lives of its students, Herbert Kohl points out that "the first and most apparent difference from their life in public school was that the students were not compelled to show up every day. No matter how much freedom exists within a public school, the teacher still must play the role of enforcer of the compulsory attendance laws. Students who don't show up are chased like criminals by truant officers and when they are caught can be sent to prison. There is no way for a teacher to feel free under this pressure. . . . Lack of compulsion is really the essence of free education."

Erickson, Donald A., ed. *Public Controls for Non-Public Schools.* Chicago: The University of Chicago Press, 1969.

This volume grew out of a national invitational conference on "State Regulation of Nonpublic Schools," occasioned by concern over the confrontation between public school officials and the Amish.

The first two chapters—the first a view of the conflict in Iowa from the governor's viewpoint, and the second from a more neutral stance—highlight the conflict between the ideal of freedom of religion and the demand for compulsory schooling. While this conflict is not resolved by the various authors, the editor concludes that "the issue of freedom of choice must be taken seriously. . . . while the public school may broaden horizons in the world of work, it is hardly a neutral forum for competing

concepts in religion, politics, economics, and other contro-
versial spheres. As a thousand battles in the courts and
elsewhere have shown, attempts to make public education
neutral in religion and in other ideological particulars
have raised problems of the profoundest sort, and the
eventual outcome of the efforts is very much in doubt."

Godwin, William. *Enquiry Concerning Political Justice and its
Influence on Morals and Happiness*, Vol 2. Toronto: The
University of Toronto Press, 1946.

Godwin was one of the first critics of compulsory schooling, well before there was any great demand for such a
policy. Such a policy, he believed, would hinder the
spread of truth because such a system has "always ex-
pended its energies in the support of prejudice; it teaches
its pupils, not the fortitude that shall bring every proposition to the test of examination, but the art of vindicating
such tenets as may chance to be established."

Compulsion was also bound to fail, he maintained, because it sought to replace a fundamental human motivation: self interest. "What I earn, what I acquire only
because I desire to acquire it, I estimate at its true value;
but what is thrust upon me, may make me indolent, but
cannot make me respectable. It is an extreme folly, to en-
deavor to secure to others, independently of exertion on
their part, the means of being happy..."

Goodman, Paul. *Compulsory Mis-Education*. New York: Hori-
zon Press, 1965.

One of the more popular critiques of compulsory schooling, and the inspiration for much of the later literature.

Goodman argues that the compulsory attendance laws
really interfere with the true education of many young
people because they are prevented from acquiring direct
experience of the world through some form of work.

The author says that the knowledge usually acquired in

the first seven years of schooling can easily be imparted in four to seven months at about the age of twelve. He also argues that we have grossly exaggerated the importance of schooling in preparing young people for a decent job. Naturally, if the corporations for foolish reasons insist that every employee have a diploma, the correlation between schooling and employment will be self-proving. Actually, with increasing automation most jobs can easily be handled by people with no extensive schooling. In General Motors' most automated plant, he points out, the average job requires only three weeks of training for people who have had no schooling whatever.

Farber, Jerry. *The Student as Nigger.* New York: Pocket Books, 1970.

Wide-ranging critique of the effects of compulsory schooling.

Farber believes that "if we want our children locked up all day until they're sixteen, let's at least be honest about it and stop trying to pass off imprisonment as education. . . .

"It would be well if we stopped lying to ourselves about what compulsory schooling does for our children. It temporarily imprisons them; it standardizes them; it intimidates them. If that's what we want we should admit it."

Gross, Ronald, and Gross, Beatrice, eds. *Radical School Reform.* Simon and Schuster, Inc., A Clarion Book, 1969.

Collection of 23 essays by most of the better known educational critics including John Holt, Paul Goodman, Jonathon Kozol, Edgar Z. Friedenbert, George Dennison, and Herbert Kohl.

Hallock, Henry Galloway. *Compulsory Education: Do We Need It?* Princeton, N.J.: Princeton University Press, 1896.

Holt, John. *Freedom and Beyond.* New York: E.P. Dutton & Co., Inc., 1972.

John Holt is among the leading critics of contemporary education. Probably his best known and most colorful criticism is his analogy of schools and jails.

In Chapter 12 of *Freedom and Beyond*, Mr. Holt wrestles with the question of compulsory schooling. First he offers what he considers the proper function of education—to promote the growth of the child. Then he criticizes education because it exploits its captive audiences (intentionally or unintentionally) to fulfil other functions, i.e., being a custodian, deciding who goes where in society, indoctrinating and being an institution of reform.

Also, he criticizes compulsory attendance as an obstacle to "feedback." When physical withdrawal is prohibited, attendance can be no measure of the teacher's success in reaching the children. Holt asserts that compulsion and education are not compatible. He offers a number of possible solutions, among them reducing the number of days that children must attend school, allowing children to select the days they wish to attend, and eliminating the laws which prohibit school-age children from "testing out" of school when they can pass the equivalency exams.

Holt, John. *The Underachieving School*. New York: Dell Publishing Co., Inc., 1969.

John Holt has emerged as one of the leading critics of the current educational scene. In this provocative collection of essays he criticizes among other things, compulsory education:

"Our compulsory school attendance laws stand in the way of good education. They should be relaxed, amended, repealed, or overturned in the courts.... The schools can be in the jail business or in the education business, but not in both....

"The laws help nobody, not the schools, not the teachers, not the children. To keep kids in school who would rather not be there costs the schools an enormous amount

of time and trouble, to say nothing of what it costs to repair the damage that these angry and resentful prisoners
do whenever they get the chance. Every teacher knows
that any kid in class who, for whatever reason, would
rather not be there, not only doesn't learn anything himself but makes learning harder for anyone else. As for
protecting the children from exploitation, the chief and
indeed only exploiters of children these days *are* the
schools....For many other kids, not going to college,
school is just a useless time-wasting obstacle preventing
them from earning needed money or doing some useful
work, or even doing some true learning."

Illich, Ivan. *Deschooling Society*. New York: Harper & Row,
Publishers, 1971.

Ivan Illich has emerged as the intellectual leader of a
band of radical educational critics advocating "deschooling society." By this they mean disestablishing
schools by abolishing compulsory attendance laws. This
slim volume of 116 pages is the chief theoretical statement of this "deschooling" movement.

Illich maintains that "all over the world the school has
an anti-educational effect on society: school is recognized
as the institution which specializes in education. The failures of school are taken by most people as a proof that
education is a very costly, very complex, always arcane,
and frequently—almost impossible task....

"School has become the world religion of a modernized
proletariat, and makes futile promises of salvation to the
poor of the technological age. The nation-state has adopted it, drafting all citizens into a graded curriculum leading to sequential diplomas not unlike the initiation rituals
and hieratic promotions of former times. The modern
state has assumed the duty of enforcing the judgment of
its educators through well-meant truant officers and job
requirements, much as did the Spanish kings who en-

forced the judgments of their theologians through the Conquistadors and the Inquisition.

"Two centuries ago the United States led the world in a movement to disestablish the monopoly of a single church. Now we need the constitutional disestablishment of the monopoly of the school, and thereby of a system which combines prejudice with discrimination. The first article of a bill of rights for a modern, humanist society would correspond to the First Amendment to the U.S. Constitution: 'The state shall make no law with respect to the establishment of education.' There shall be no ritual obligatory for all."

See also Ohlinger below.

Katz, Michael B. *The Irony of Early School Reform: Educational Innovation in Mid-Nineteenth Century Massachusetts.* Boston: Beacon Press, 1968.

The spread of first state schools and then compulsory attendance laws during the last century is usually depicted as a great victory of the common people in their quest for a better life. Professor Katz shows from a study of New England that the facts were nearly the opposite of this popular myth. He shows that the demand for secondary schooling came from a social and economic elite, and that it was opposed by the poorer elements of the population. Thus he says:

"But the establishment of the public high schools, as we have seen, did little to promote the mobility of the lowest social groups.... By stressing that high schools were democratic, that they fostered equality of opportunity, educational promoters could cover personal motives with the noblest of sentiments. What they were doing was spreading throughout the whole community the burden of educating a small minority of its children."

He concludes:

"Very simply, the extension and reform of education in

the mid-nineteenth century were not a potpourri of democracy, nationalism, and humanitarianism. They were the attempt of a coalition of social leaders, status-anxious parents, and status-hungry educators to impose educational innovation, each for their own reasons, upon a reluctant community."

Mill, John Stuart. *On Liberty* 1859. Chicago: Henry Regnery Company—A Gateway Edition, 1955.

This essay by Mill—inspired by Wilhelm von Humbolt's *The Sphere and Duties of Government*—has rightly been esteemed as one of the classics of liberty. While Mill did believe in a form of compulsory education he was opposed to state education or even compulsory schooling. "A general state education," he believed, "is a mere contrivance for moulding people to be exactly like one another; and as the mould in which it casts them is that which pleases the predominant power in the government— whether this be a monarch, a priesthood, an aristocracy, or the majority of the existing generation—in proportion as it is efficient and successful, it establishes a despotism over the mind, leading by natural tendency to one over the body."

Montgomery, Zach. *Poison Drops in the Federal Senate. The School Question from a Parental and Non-Sectarian Standpoint.* 1886. Houston: St. Thomas Press, N.D.

The only booklength critique of compulsory state-schooling as a denial of parental rights.

In addition, the author, by comparing the several states with histories of compulsory schooling with other states in which it had only recently been adopted, shows that in per capita terms the former have six times the number of criminals, twice the number of paupers, twice the number of insane, and four times the number of suicides. He further shows, through an examination of ten different states, that criminality rose as expenditure on state-schooling increased.

Neill, A. S. *Summerhill: A Radical Approach to Child Rearing*. New York: Hart Publishing Company, 1960.

An exposition of the philosophy behind and operation of this famous school.

"Summerhill is the name of a small school, but it signifies a great experiment in education. In the forty years of its existence its founder has proved. . .one simple truth—*freedom works*." Sir Herbert Read.

"Here is a man who has had the courage to be what he believes: and what he believes is that children best become self-regulated individuals in an atmosphere of love, trust, understanding and responsible freedom. Consequently he has dropped from his school all such concepts as coercion, compulsion, authority, obedience. . ." Carl R. Rogers.

DuPont de Nemours, Pierre S. *National Education in the United States*. Newark, Delaware: University of Delaware Press, 1923.

Written in 1800, this study is of value for the evidence it contains of widespread literacy in the United States long before schooling was either compulsory or state-supported. "Most young Americans," he found, "can read, write and cipher. Not more than four in a thousand are unable to write legibly—even neatly. . . .

"In America a great many people read the Bible, and all the people read a newspaper.... And as the newspapers of the United States are filled with all sort of narratives—comments on matters, political, physical, philosophic; information on agriculture, the arts, travel, navigation; and also extracts from all the best books in America and Europe—they disseminate an enormous amount of information, some of which is helpful to the young people, especially when they arrive at an age when the father resigns his place as reader in favor of the child who can best succeed him."

Nutting, Willis. *Schools and the Means of Education.* Notre Dame, Ind.: Fides Publishing Assn., 1959.

This little book (126 pp.), published more than a decade ago, makes a strong case for the "de-schooling" of society by, among other things, the repeal of compulsory school attendance laws: "The fundamental laws which support the present conception of education are the laws compelling attendance at school. Never was there a system of laws with more noble intent. But few laws have had results more questionable. They have turned out to be a very great blow struck at our youth, for they have made a portion of our young people spend years of their time in an environment altogether unsuited to them, and by making the schools take these people they have transformed the schools into institutions that can't do the best work for the portion that really belong in school.... the laws have actually fenced hundreds of thousands of children into a concentration camp for some of the most formative years of their lives."

Professor Nutting argues that much worthwhile education which cannot be acquired in a classroom can be acquired in the home or in some form of gainful employment.

Ohlinger, John, and McCarthy, Colleen. *Lifelong Learning or Lifelong Schooling? A Tentative View of the Ideas of Ivan Illich With a Quotational Bibliography.* Syracuse, N.Y.: Syracuse University Publications in Continuing Education, 1972.

See also Illich above.

Read, Leonard E. *Anything That's Peaceful: The Case for the Free Market.* Irvington-on-Hudson, N.Y.: The Foundation for Economic Education, 1964.

Compulsion is totally out of place in education according to Leonard Reed because "education is a seeking, probing, taking-from process, and the initiative must rest with the seeker." And, by contrast, "Coercion, clearly, is not a creative force; it is, by definition, repressive and destructive. Physical force can no more be used to stimulate the spirit of inquiry or advance wisdom or expand consciousness or increase perception than it can be employed to improve prayer—and for precisely the same reason. Acquiring understanding or wisdom springs from the volitional faculty. . ."

Read, Leonard. *Government—An Ideal Concept.* Irvington-on-Hudson, N.Y.: Foundation for Economic Education, 1954.

The author maintains that the present educational system based on compulsory attendance and compulsory tax support is not only immoral, but unproductive. He believes that in the absence of this compulsion we would have a flourishing educational system, and that the "good work being done in government education is in spite of, not because of aggressive force."

Reimer, Everett. *School Is Dead: Alternatives In Education,* Garden City, N.Y.: Doubleday & Company, Inc., 1971.

This book is the result of a discussion the author has carried on over the past fifteen years with Ivan Illich, especially during the past five years as director of the seminar on Alternatives in Education hosted each year at CIDOC in Cuernavaca. As a result, the author's analysis and prescriptions are very similar to those offered by Illich in *Deschooling Society.*

Compulsory schooling, Reimer maintains, is damaging because it fails to educate those subject to it, and, in fact, makes learning difficult if not impossible because it seeks to promote learning in the absence of real interest and in an environment foreign to the student's world. He also charges that it holds its young charges in a state of needlessly prolonged childhood, and that it necessarily conditions them to an unthinking acceptance of the politico-economic status quo.

See especially chapters 1-5.

Rothbard, Murray N. *Education, Free and Compulsory*, Center for Independent Education, 1972.

In this essay, Dr. Rothbard surveys the history of compulsory education in Europe and America and traces the influence of European educators upon the development of education in America.

Historically, he points out, the schools have been the tool of either the church or state. When the former has been in control the schools were used to promote sectarian doctrines and moral codes. When the state controlled them, the schools have been used to mold an obedient citizenry. In either case, the growth and development of the individual were denied.

The author also discusses the importance of realizing the unique and individual character of the learner. "The lack of equality—in tastes, ability and character—is not necessarily an invidious distinction, it simply reflects the scope of human diversity. Enthusiasm for equality should actually be viewed as anti-human. It tends to repress the flowering of individual personality and diversity, and, indeed, of civilization itself. . ."

"The key issue," Rothbard asserts, "is simply this: shall the parent or the state be the overseer of the child? . . .There is no middle ground in this issue. One or the other must exercise ultimate control, and no third party with authority to seize the child and rear it has been found."

Rushdoony, Rousas J. *The Messianic Character of American Education*. Nutley, N.J.: The Craig Press, 1963.

This root-and-branch attack on compulsory state-schooling is particularly valuable in demonstrating the messianic character of the claims made for state schooling by its leading advocates.

The author holds that the logic of compulsory state education leads to full socialization, for "statist education is the socialization of the child. If the state can own and socialize our children, then it can most certainly own and socialize our property. We cannot legitimately surrender our children to the state and its schools and then claim the right to withhold our property. The major concession makes the objection to the lesser absurd, and an instance of misplaced values."

Contains brief biographical and bibliographical sketches of leading educationists.

Seybolt, Robert Francis. *Apprenticeship & Apprenticeship Education in Colonial New England & New York*. New York: Teacher's College, Columbia University, 1917.

"In New England and New York the first laws concerning education, and the first compulsory education laws were contained in apprenticeship enactments. As we have seen, the apprenticeship system took care of the entire problem of public elementary education during the colonial period."

Brief, straightforward account based on contemporary documents.

Seybolt, Robert Francis. *The Private Schools of Colonial Boston*. Cambridge, Mass.: Harvard University Press, 1935.

Brief account based on extensive contemporary documentation, and of considerable value in that it shows the variety and sophistication of the educational services offered prior to the introduction of compulsory attendance.

"The records of the private schools tell a story which is quite different from that of the public schools. Unhampered by the control of the town meeting, and little influenced by traditional modes of procedure, these institutions were free to grow with the town. This they did as conditions suggested it. The result was a remarkably comprehensive program of instruction which appears to have met every contemporary educational need....

"The public schools made no attempt to meet the educational needs of all. They continued in their old accustomed ways. The private schools were free to originate, and to adopt their courses of instruction to the interests of the students. The masters sought always to keep strictly abreast of the time, for their livelihood depended on the success with which they met these needs. No such freedom or incentive was offered the masters of the public schools. It is quite evident that the private school was a flexible, growing institution which played an important part in the educational life of the town."

Seybolt, Robert Francis. *The Public Schools of Colonial Boston, 1635-1775.* Cambridge, Mass.: Harvard University Press, 1935.

Brief, objective treatment based on a mass of contemporary documentation.

Small, Walter. *Early New England Schools*. Boston: Ginn and Company, Publishers, 1914.

Useful history based largely on the official records of the towns, colonies and states, local histories and the publications of historical and genealogical societies.

Shows the widespread private provision of education prior to the time it was made compulsory.

Contains bibliography.

Spencer, Herbert. *Social Statics* 1851. New York: Robert Schallkenbach Foundation, 1954.

> Spencer's first major—and perhaps finest—work in which his theoretical and practical objections to compulsory state schooling are very persuasively presented. He points out that the child's rights are not violated by the parent's failure to provide schooling; that in order for the state to compel schooling it becomes necessary for the state to define education, thus destroying educational variety, and that because of political self-interest, such schooling must inevitably be statist in nature.

Spencer, Herbert. *The Principles of Ethics.* Vol. 1. New York: P. Appleton & Co., 1892.

> The author maintains that compulsory attendance or state provision of schooling are a violation of parental rights and responsibilities and hence ethically inadmissible.
> "We have fallen upon evil times, in which it has come to be an accepted doctrine that part of the responsibilities are to be discharged not by the parents but by the public . . . Agitators and legislators have united in spreading a theory which, logically followed out, ends in the monstrous conclusion that it is for parents to beget children and for society to take care of them. The political ethics now in fashion makes the unhesitating assumption that while each man, as parent, is not responsible for the mental culture of his own offspring, he is, as citizen, along with other citizens, responsible for the mental culture of all other men's offspring."

Spring, Joel H. *Education and the Rise of the Corporate State.* Boston: Beacon Press, 1972.

> An "examination of the roots of the modern state school system and the motives of the major figures who moulded its present shape....," says R. A. Childs Jr.

"Spring finds that it was under the influence of liberals during the Progressive era that public schools began to take their modern shape, when both intellectuals and businessmen alike became suddenly 'social minded' and concerned with managing the private lives of factory workers and citizens.

"The classroom gradually became the focus of those who wanted to shape, not just the lives of immigrants and factory workers, but of entire generations. The goal became to mould peoples' characters, and a major goal explicitly became to use the classroom as a tool for producing good factory workers fit for assembly lines.

"Spring's book goes beyond this, however, to investigate the rise of the doctrine which held that the purpose of state education was to establish 'social control' over children, moulding them into whatever type of citizen happened to be politically in favor at the time."

Stephen, Sir Leslie. *The English Utilitarians*, 3 vols. in 1. 1900. New York: Peter Smith and Co., 1950.

This classic work on this subject contains useful information on the private educational activities in England prior to the establishment of compulsory rate-supported schools.

Stirner, Max. *The False Principle of our Education*, 1842. Colorado Springs: Ralph Myles Publisher, 1967.

An intrepid and uncompromising defense of the individual and his will against the compulsory schooling of his time. Stirner believed that much of what passes for education was largely worthless because it has no relationship to the students' own will. As a result, "Our good background of recalcitrancy gets strongly suppressed and with it the development of knowledge to free will. The result of school life then is philistinism. . .If one awakens in men the idea of freedom then the free men will incessantly go on to free themselves; if on the contrary, one only *educates* them, then they will at all times accommodate themselves to circumstances in the *most highly educated and elegant manner* and degenerate into subservient cringing souls."

von Humbolt, Wilhelm. *The Limits of State Action.* Cambridge, England: Cambridge University Press, 1969.

In this classic essay von Humbolt stated that "the grand, the leading principle, toward which every argument unfolded in these pages directly converges, is the absolute and essential importance of human development in its widest diversity." It was this principle which caused the author to say that "education seems to me to lie wholly beyond the limits within which political agency should be properly confined." Compulsory education would be harmful because it would necessarily attempt to mould everyone according to a common pattern rather than allowing a natural diversity to flower.

Weber, Samuel Edwin. *The Charity School Movement in Colonial Pennsylvania.* Philadelphia: Press of G. F. Lasher, 1905.

West, E. G. *Education and the State.* London: Institute for Economic Affairs, 1955.

This volume issued by the eminent Institute for Economic Affairs in London is undoubtedly the best overall treatment of the economic arguments in favor of state education. According to the author, neither the "protection of minors" principle nor the argument from "neighborhood effects" are adequate to justify state provision of education on the present "socialized" or "nationalized" pattern.

The evidence presented from the nineteenth century shows that even in the absence of compulsory attendance laws and state provision of "free" schools, English parents were providing education for their children, that over two-thirds were literate and that the net effect of the introduction of state education was to stifle this healthy, natural growth.

II—Articles

Berger, Herbert, M.D., F.A.C.P. "Compulsory Education: A Cause of Drug Addiction." *Medical Times* 97 (1969): 178-182.

The author, after an extensive study of drug users, found that "one factor stands out in almost all these interviews. It was an absolute hatred of '*compulsory education*'! This symptom was noted by the patients early in primary school and became full blown by the age of 12."

He concludes that "compulsory education engenders in the uneducable, a hatred of society. In the expression of this antipathy the adolescent repudiates his culture. He attempts to destroy his jail and his neighbor's property. Finally he attempts a chemical escape from the vicissitudes of his environment."

Bien, Bettina. "Today's School Problem" in *Essays on Liberty*. Irvington-on-Hudson, N.Y.: Foundation for Economic Education, 1958, vol. 5.

A brief historical review of the origins of state education in the United States. The author concludes that experience with our government school system has raised serious doubts as to the suitability of force to serve the cause of true education. "Therefore, why not consider removing government restraints on individual initiative in that field?" She specifically suggests the repeal of compulsory attendance laws. "Many of the troublemakers responsible for the greatest share of the teachers' disciplinary problems would be glad to leave school for jobs where they

ld begin to feel useful to themselves and to the
rld... Once more the responsibility for a child's educa-
ɔn and discipline would be recognized as belonging to
the parents."

Carle, Erica, "Education Without Taxation." *Freeman*, March
1962, pp. 48-55

Most Americans today believe that prior to the provision
of full state schooling very few children were educated,
and that should the state cease its activity in this field
most youngsters would again remain uneducated. Actually, the truth is almost the reverse of this. The nineteenth
century was an age of great concern for education and a
time of great experimentation. The article interestingly
relates the story of one of the most promising and successful of these experiments.

Joseph Lancaster, a Quaker teacher, opened his first
school for the poor in London in 1798 at the age of twenty. He began by teaching the essentials of the subjects to a
few of the most promising lads and then making them
monitors with the responsibility of devoting part of their
time to teaching a class of ten younger scholars. Under
this arrangement Lancaster was able to take charge of up
to 1,000 pupils.

Unfortunately, the school's startling success made it an
attractive prize for those seeking the imposition of a particular religious orthodoxy and for pedagogs who felt hu-
miliated in being reduced to the supervision of "transient,
ignorant, and unskilled monitors." And finally with the
rise of state education, the economy possible under such a
plan no longer seemed necessary or even desirable.

"Compulsory Attendance Is Futile; School Administrators
Opinion Poll." *Nation's Schools* 65 (May, 1960): 70 ff.

Results of poll show most administrators against rigid enforcement of compulsory attendance.

Davidson, Thomas. "Education" in *The Encyclopaedia of Social Reform*. New York: Funk and Wagnalls Company, 1897, pp. 520-540.

Objectively written article treating the nature and history of education from ancient times to the late nineteenth century. Contains extensive statistical data on school attendance in both the United States and in Europe. Contains brief statement of the individualist case against compulsory, state schooling.

Godwin, William. "On the Communication of Knowledge," in *The Enquirer: Reflections on Education, Manners, and Literature*. Dublin: J. Moore, 1797, pp. 76-83. Reprinted in Krimerman, Leonard I., and Perry, Lewis: *Patterns of Anarchy: A Collection of Books on the Anarchist Tradition*, Garden City, N.Y.: Anchor Books—Doubleday & Company, Inc., 1966, pp. 421-425.

Godwin was a foe of compulsory schooling not only for political reasons but because he believed compulsion to be antithetical to the learning process. "Liberty," he wrote, "is one of the most desirable of all sublunary advantages. I would therefore communicate knowledge without infringing, or with as little as possible violence to, the volition and individual judgment of the person to be instructed....

"Is it necessary that a child should learn a thing before it can have any idea of its value?...The true object of juvenile education is to provide against the age of five-and-twenty a mind well regulated, active and prepared to learn. Whatever will inspire habits of industry and observation will sufficiently answer this purpose....Study with desire is real activity; without desire it is but the semblance and mockery of activity."

Greer, Colin, "Public Schools: The Myth of the Melting Pot." *Saturday Review of Literature*, November 1969, p. 84.

A penetrating article adapted from the author's book *Cobweb Attitudes: Essays in American Education and Culture* in which he insists that "the public schools have always failed the lower classes—both white and black. Current educational problems stem not from the fact that the schools have changed, but from the fact that they continue to do precisely the job they have always done."

The author is refreshingly candid in his discussion of compulsory attendance and its relationship to efficiency which "was measured by the success schools had in getting more youngsters into the classroom, almost never by academic success or lack of it. The ratio of the number of children in school to the number in the community who ought legally to be in attendance was the measure, and academic success was by no means a necessary concomitant."

Effectively disposes of the myth that the state schools have aided socio-economic mobility.

Holt, John. "Deschooling Society." *Reason*, April-May 1971, pp. 14-17.

Using an analysis originated by Ivan Illich, Holt argues that by confusing education with schooling we have made it artificially scarce—and expensive—as well as excessively mysterious.

The author also proposes "granting children virtually all the rights and privileges and prerogatives and responsibilities and duties which we grant to adults.... The right to direct your own learning and your own life."

James, E. J., "Compulsory Education." *Encyclopaedia of Political Science, Political Economy and of the Political History of the United States,* ed. James J. Lalor. New York: Charles E. Merrill Co., 1888. Vol. 2, pp. 41-48.

A brief survey of compulsory education as adopted in Europe during the 18th and 19th centuries.

The article is significant in that author while clearly favoring compulsory education still admits that "it is safe to say that it is easier to prove that the state has the right to compel attendance of its children at school than to show that such a policy is generally successful, in the widest sense of the term, and therefore expedient." He says further that "recent compulsory school laws in America have been chiefly remarkable for their utter failure to accomplish any of the results expected of them. Of the twenty-two American states and territories which have compulsory laws on their statute books, not a single one has been able to report 'they are a success.' The same thing is true of similar laws in many other countries. The fact seems to be that compulsory school laws on a large scale have been successful only under conditions which would have made a voluntary system of attendance a success."

The extent of public support for compulsory attendance laws may be garnered from the author's admission that "there is not a single section of our country where the public sentiment in favor of such a law is strong enough to secure its enforcement by the local authorities.... Local enforcement is generally a dead letter, and the most utterly dead exactly where it is most needed, viz., in illiterate communities."

Johnson, Thomas. "The Foundation of Freedom." *Reason*, April-May 1971, pp. 6-12.

Professor Johnson argues that because of its compulsory nature our present schools are educationally destructive. He calls for the abolition of "the children's prisons, the schools...leaving each child free to develop his own mind, according to his own interests, at his own rate of speed, in a psychologically healthy environment."

Kay, Robert E., M.D. "Our American Educational System: Do So-Called Modern Schools Do More Harm Than Good?," *Clinical Pediatrics* 8 (1969): 548-555.

The author—chief of Children's Services at the Philadelphia Psychiatric Center—suggests that on the whole our compulsory schooling exerts a poor influence on most students, and that for some they may be positively destructive.

"Most of our school children are working apathetically and fearfully far below their capacity. In addition they are in no way being prepared for adult life where they will be free to choose their job, be allowed to resign, and where they will receive usable rewards for performing well....

"The essence of maturity is one's ability to make an appropriate choice. School children are given virtually no meaningful opportunity to practice this skill. The government or school system controls attendance, class placement, seating, movement and to a very large degree even talk.

"The student who fails to adapt to this imposed and arbitrary set of demands is labelled deviant. He may then be stigmatized by counseling, psychological evaluation, psychiatric treatment or special education."

Landes, William M., and Solmon, Lewis C., "Compulsory Schooling Legislation: An Economic Analysis of Law and Social Change in the Nineteenth Century." *The Journal of Economic History 32* (1972): 54-91.

Professors Landes and Solmon deny that legislation and related efforts at social reform have significantly altered behavior. In regard to education, they argue that compulsory school attendance laws are nearly meaningless, if not harmful. The authors contend that the basic question remains unanswered: what has been the effect, if any, of these laws on school enrolment and attendance?

Among the Northern states, only two had compulsory attendance laws prior to 1870. Within thirty years, all Northern states had laws compelling attendance. A very similar situation existed in the South just thirty years later. By 1900, only two Southern states had compulsory schooling laws and, within two decades, all had them.

Professors Landes and Sol'mon examine these two models and offer the evidence as a challenge to the popular notion that compulsory school attendance legislation is responsible for literacy in this country.

Machan, Tibor. "The Schools Ain't What They Used To Be And Never Was," *Reason*, April-May 1971, pp. 23-29.

An able examination of the philosophical and psychological consequences of compulsory attendance laws and state financed schooling.

Nelson, John O. "Compulsory Schooling," *Reason*, April-May 1971, pp. 19-20.

Professor Nelson believes that the strongest claim for compulsory attendance laws is that in their absence "children, by and large, would not learn to read and write." He presents historical evidence that in the absence of such laws in the early years of our history children, by and large, did learn to read and write even though school attendance was not required.

The strongest case that can be made *against* compulsory schooling, he believes, "is certainly the argument that compulsory school attendance induces juvenile delinquency, crime and drug addiction." And he presents evidence from both the English and American scenes to the effect that that is, in fact, its result.

Nelson, John. "Displaced Persons, Dyspepsia, and Disaster," mimeographed. Menlo Park, Calif.: Institute for Humane Studies, Inc., 1969.

Professor Nelson argues that compulsory school attendance laws have effectively displaced most young people from doing what they ordinarily would be doing, i.e., earning a livelihood in gainful employment.

This displacement, he argues, is the cause of the frustration and dyspepsia so many suffer, because they are effectively divorced from reality and forced to spend years at something all but the smallest fraction have no talent for — the manipulation of symbols and abstractions. And, he tells us, "When he graduates from this training he has not acquired or developed the physical and psychological powers involved in working directly upon reality, as in carpentry or operating a lathe. . . . If forced into the production or servicing of physical commodities, he finds himself to be inept, psychologically dissatisfied, and disoriented. Thus, he has been displaced — not temporarily but permanently."

Nelson, John O. "Two Main Evils of Formal Education," (unpublished manuscript. Boulder, Colorado: University of Colorado).

Nelson, John O. "The University and Secondary Education." *Freeman,* December 1967, pp. 724-731.

Professor Nelson advocates the removal of tax support and compulsory attendance laws from secondary schooling on the grounds that by and large they *unfit* young persons for life:

"What, then, is the outcome if . . . almost the entire population of the young is forced to attend schools devoted to the preliminaries of university education? We can expect to find, and we do find, a large percentage of young persons who have been trained mentally, physically, and emotionally to do and be what they are not suited to do or be. More tragic, though these young persons have learned in the process, or will have learned, to consider alien or even contemptible those very things that most of them were naturally suited to be and do."

Pearson, George. "The Case Against Education Vouchers." *Reason,* April-May 1971, pp. 35-36

> Though widely viewed as a step toward educational freedom and diversity, the adoption of an educational vouchers scheme, would, in fact, mean the loss of the independence of the existing independent schools according to the author.
>
> Even Christopher Jencks, the author points out, recognizes the possibility of the agency regulating the use of vouchers evolving into a political force strong enough to result in a "regulatory agency as complex and detailed as that now governing the public schools . . . they (the schools receiving the vouchers) would probably end up indistinguishable from existing public schools."

Perrin, John William, "Beginnings in Compulsory Education." *Educational Review* 25 (1903): 240-248.

Perrin, John William, "Compulsory Education in New England, 1850-1890." *Journal of Pedagogy* 17 (1905): 261-276.

Poole, Robert, Jr. "The Case for Education Vouchers." *Reason*, April-May 1971, pp. 30-34.

> Education vouchers, the author argues would have a number of beneficial results, among them, getting people to view education as a service—"something to be selected and purchased in response to one's particular needs," getting parents to think more actively of their responsibilities because of the necessity to make choices; and, in the long run, the disestablishment of the government educational establishment.

Reynolds, J. "Children's Privacy and Compulsory Schooling." *Teacher's College Record* 68 (1966): 33-41.

> Thoughtful article prompted by realization that compulsory schooling involved a violation of the child's right to privacy, as well as several other rights.

Snoody, J. L. "Let's Let Them Go." *California Journal of Secondary Education* 33 (1958): 119-122.

Spring, Joel H. "Anarchism and Education: The Dissenting Tradition." *Libertarian Analysis*, December 1971, pp. 30-42.

This brief article, based on a paper first published by the Center for Intercultural Documentation (CIDOC), Cuernavaca, Mexico, surveys the writings of Godwin, Ferrer, Stirner, Tolstoy, and Emma Goldman critical of compulsory state schooling.

Spring, Joel H., "Education and the Rise of the Corporate State." *Socialist Revolution*, March-April 1972, pp. 73-101.

Scholarly article showing how compulsory schooling evolved during the nineteenth and twentieth centuries in response to changing conceptions of the economic order. He concludes that "by the middle of the twentieth century the one-sided contest had apparently ended and the public school was unchallenged as the primary instrument for socialization in the United States."

West, E. G., "The Political Economy of American Public School Legislation." *The Journal of Law and Economics 10* (1967): 101-128.

Professor West gives us an account of the dual consideration of compulsory payment and compulsory consumption legislation as it evolved in New York during the nineteenth century.

Dr. West points out that until the free school campaign got underway in the 1840s, it seems to have been readily acknowledged that education could continue to be universal without being gratuitous and without compulsion. In 1866, the year before the abolition of the rate bills (fees to the parents who were required to pay in proportion to the attendance of their children) in New York, education continued to be almost universal, although not yet compulsory.

West maintains that "the final link" in the process of monopolizing education for the state occurred in New York with the passage of the Compulsory Education Act in 1874.

West, E. G., "Private versus Public Education—A Classical Economic Dispute." *Journal of Political Economy LXXII* (1964): 465-75.

In the author's words he first offers "a brief description of the school and university situation during the time of Adam Smith. Next I shall examine Smith's preference in his own circumstances for the operation of market forces in providing education. I shall then sketch the development of government policy in education over the subsequent century showing the roles of J. S. Mill, Nassau Senior, and Edwin Chadwick. Finally, I contrast the ideas of Robert Lowe, the last true representative of Adam Smith on education with the dominant ideas of his contemporaries, Mills, Senior and Chadwick."

West, E. G. "Social Legislation and the Demand for Children: Comment." *Western Economic Journal* 6 (1969): 419-424.
In this comment, Professor West cautions against an uncritical belief that compulsory schooling legislation played a substantial part in promoting schooling and literacy in 19th and early 20th century England. He points out that "at least in the eyes of the political legislators the coercive elements of the English Education Act of 1870 were openly directed not to a majority but to a minority of 'delinquent' families." On the basis of the quite compelling evidence he cites for the continuing, voluntary growth of education prior to such legislation he believes that it is indeed difficult to extricate the true behavioral influence of compulsion per se. Meanwhile we can antici-

pate that at one extreme, if collectivization of education turns out to be only a summing of the private economic and educational circumstances of families, "compulsion will emerge as merely a kind of symbol of aggregated aspiration."

West, E. G. "Subsidized But Compulsory Consumption Goals: Some Special Welfare Cases," *Kyklos—International Review for Social Sciences* 24 (1971): 535-545.

The author, in this article, seeks to assess "the degree of complementarity and substitutability between lump-sum grants, price subsidies and legal compulsion" with a particular focus in the area of schooling. He concludes that "normally price subsidies paid for by Group B are the most efficient method available to encourage further consumption of a good by Group A. However, beyond a point, if Group A suffers negative utility from marginal consumption, Group B may be able be overcome this obstacle by offering an additional *income* subsidy." The use of compulsion is shown to be of only marginal value in most such instances.